Interpersonal Communication in Organizational Settings

Communication Skills for Business and Professional Success

Michael Spangle, Ph.D.
Jacqueline Moorhead, Ph.D.
University of Denver

KENDALL/HUNT PUBLISHING COMPANY
4050 Westmark Drive   Dubuque, Iowa 52002

Contents

Chapter Four
Developing Communication Competencies

Chapter Five
Communication Channels between Supervisors and Employees

Chapter Six
Communication with Peers

Chapter Seven
Communication on Teams

Chapter Eight
Communication with Crazymakers

Chapter Nine
Difficult Organizational Settings

Chapter Ten
Learning Individuals in Learning Organizations

References

Index

ACKNOWLEDGMENTS

The goal for this book was to integrate some of the best insights from communication research with communication principles currently used by successful professionals. Drawn from a wide range of industries, these professionals demonstrate the many settings in which effective communication principles can be applied. We gratefully acknowledge the important contributions of the following people who shared their time and insights with us:

Sue Baker - communications

Ramie Becker - marketing

Janie Chambers - sales

Bill Chapman - telecommunications

Mary Colton - recreation

Peter Garcia - police department

Katharine Grant - student services

Lisa Hughes - computer consulting firm

Dan Johnson - manufacturing

Lavonne Johnson - family therapy

John Mayer - airline pilot

John Pinelli - communications

Milt Robinson - U S Forest Service

Vicki Siegel-Makowa - health care

Joe Stasik - U S Information Agency

Garry Woody - aerospace

Nadia Younes - human resources

In addition, we deeply appreciate the invaluable encouragement and contributions of our copy editors, Linda Spangle, a writer who works in the health care industry, and Laura Buseman Ph.D., a professor in English at Black Hills State University. These two shared their wonderful talent for clarifying and explaining by translating many of our complex concepts into words that can be more easily understood.

INTRODUCTION

I am interested in the future because I will spend the rest of my life there.

C.F. Kettery, *Seeds for Thought*

As we move toward the next decade, organizations on every level of society are looking for effective ways to deal with multiple and complex changes. We use many terms to describe the challenges, such as restructuring, re-engineering, hyperturbulence, and rightsizing. Organizations face the loss of continuity with the past as they endure the changes. They face the challenge of integrating new communication technologies with existing procedures.

The growing edge of organizational communication moves beyond discussion of how individuals and groups communicate to a new frontier where we discuss how organizations as communities communicate. Borrowing from computer terminology, we might describe the new interpersonal dynamics as the *organizational web* where people, their leaders, and processes relate in an interlocking web of systems. The choices about how we communicate and with whom we communicate influence the web. The morale in one department has the potential to affect morale of other departments. Relationships within the organization can influence the organization's success in the community. Thus, organizational members are in small ways both part of the problem and part of the solution. In the organizational web, the quality and morale of the community will be dependent upon organizational members who consistently do the following:

- Participate in a learning environment through the develop ment of essential communication competencies. These competencies enable members to communicate effectively at all levels of the organization.
- Demonstrate a commitment to collaboration. The American cultural trend is toward greater use of project teams in organizational processes.

- Develop an awareness that communication involves choices. Communication is shaped and adapted based on observation of its effectiveness in achieving goals and building relationships.
- Contribute to decision making, problem solving, and information sharing processes, as if relationships mattered. How we deal with people today will affect our success tomorrow.

During the next decade, the impact of electronic technologies on organizational communication is likely to increase in magnitude. Information will be processed faster and in greater quantity. The greater flow of information about environmental needs and possibilities will make organizational decisions more complex and require more effective team processes. As organizations become more interlinked with communities, regionally, nationally, and globally, they'll need to develop more sophisticated communication processes to meet demands. Throughout the growth and changes, interpersonal communication will assume a greater role. Electronic communication supplements one-to-one and group communication, it does not replace it. The demand for clarity, interpretation, and meaning will never cease to be important. Workers must develop powerful skills for conquering the challenges presented by difficult people and difficult situations. This book will help you build those skills, add to them, and encourage you to teach them to others.

CHAPTER ONE

Communication
Drives Our Lives

The most important thing I learned in school was how to communicate. You can have brilliant ideas, but if you can't get them across, your brains won't get you anywhere.
-Lee Iacocca, *Iacocca*

Improving communication skills – Why bother?

Most of us can probably think of any number of excuses not to work on our communication skills. Learning new skills or improving old ones can require much time and energy, so considering how busy we already are, why should we invest our time in this particular area?

Promotions and other rewards may seem to be linked more to technical knowledge and achievements than to the ability to work with people. In fact, employees who work in isolated settings, such as computer programmers or accountants, may feel that they never see other workers, so why bother learning communication skills? In addition, many workers tend to believe that their communication skills are good enough already, in spite of occasional feedback to the contrary.

The power of communication

The truth is that being able to communicate effectively can powerfully influence your work as well as your relationships. By improving your ability to articulate clearly and connect with your listener, you can enhance your credibility, improve your problem-solving skills, and increase your effectiveness in leading a work team. From a practical stand-point, communication excellence helps you:

- Become more successful in dealing with people who drive you crazy
- Create better outcomes when you experience conflict with other people
- Develop greater confidence for working in groups
- Improve your relationships with friends, family and colleagues
- Manage the dynamics of difficult situations more effectively

Changing communication expectations

In the business world, managers frequently identify communication skills as one of the most valued abilities in employees. For example, in a study conducted by AT&T, managing interpersonal relationships was listed as one of the most significant skills for leaders of the future (Stahl, 1989).

Like managers, staff workers also express the need for more knowledge and ability in communicating. In a University of Michigan study, more than 70% of respondents identified business communication courses as being more helpful than classes in accounting, finance, or marketing in preparing them for their careers (Heckel, 1987). Many companies view communication competence as so important that they have instituted training programs, or partnered with educational institutions to improve worker's communication skills (O'Hair & Friedrich, 1992).

Even fields that have historically required a high level of technical skills with minimal people interaction are now changing their job descriptions to include more interpersonal skills. For example, professionals in human resource departments have seen much of their technical work become accessible through personal computers, networks, and the Internet. This means they now spend more of their time doing consulting and project management, work that requires a higher level of interpersonal skills than writing computer programs. "They must avoid conveying the image of someone who wants to be locked in a room and have floppy disks slipped under the door so they can be alone with the computer" (Cottell & Robertson, 1987, p. 114).

Another area of change involves the increased use of microcomputers in organizations. Employees who provide technical support increasingly look for team members who are people-oriented. Testing and evaluating hardware and software has expanded to include training users and helping solve their problems. The technician's ability to communicate affects how easily information is translated into user-friendly terms that the non-technical employee can comprehend.

To survive in our current corporate world, workers will be expected to develop greater communication versatility. They must become effective not only with one-on-one communication, but also in small group (team) and technology-based forms of communication. Adrian (1994), editor of *Manufacturing Automation*, reports that senior executives from some of the United States' leading manufacturing companies agree that future success in manufacturing will require balancing new technologies with human skills, such as continuous learning and knowledge-building. To manage change effectively, manufacturing will emphasize leadership, motivational, and interpersonal skills as well as technical capabilities.

What is communication?

Although communication is one of the most basic human activities, it is a difficult process to define. A wide range of scholarly definitions include the following:

> The transmission of information, emotions, skills, etc. by the use of symbols such as words, pictures, graphs, and so on. It is the act or process of transmission that is usually called communication. (Berelson & Steiner, 1964, p. 527)

> A process where people influence each other. (Infante, Rancer, & Womack, 1990, p. 13)

> A transactional process of exchanging messages and negotiating meaning to convey information and to establish and maintain relationships. (Wilson, Hantz, & Hanna, 1995, p. 4)

Most of us recognize good communication when we see it, but we may not be able to explain what makes it effective. Similarly, we generally know when there is an absence of good communication, but we may not recognize what should be changed to improve it. Communication involves a process of listening and responding, give-and-take, negotiating meaning, and exchanging information, so that people can achieve their goals.

We cannot *not* communicate

Even when we think we are not communicating, we are still sending messages to the people around us. According to Watzlawick, Bavelas and Jackson (1967), all behaviors may be interpreted and assigned meaning as forms of communication. These authors believe it impossible to *not* communicate. When a co-worker sits at a computer, focuses intently on the screen, and ignores the activity going on in the hallway or other offices, his or her behavior sends the message, "Leave me alone; I can't be bothered right now."

A scowling colleague who stands with arms crossed during a discussion sends a clear negative message. Because communication is thus continual, we need to be aware of the messages we continuously send, both intentionally or unintentionally, if we are to be effective communicators.

Communication and human needs

Communication helps fulfill and satisfy many of our basic needs. We gather information to help us with decisions. We ask questions to reduce uncertainty or to clarify what we don't understand. We grow and are challenged intellectually as we talk about issues. Communication scholars Ron Adler and Neil Towne (1987) identify four sets of needs that are addressed by communication:

1. *Physical needs*
   Research has shown that individuals who lack contact with others experience higher risk of physical or mental illness. In fact, severe interpersonal deprivation has been correlated in some children with the development of autism. Lack of adult conversation and friendship can make us more vulnerable to burnout. When we are facing stressful situations or events, reducing isolation improves our ability to cope. Some days it takes a lot of work to maintain our interpersonal relationships, but if the interactions are positive ones, they can make a significant contribution to our physical well-being.

2. *Identity needs*
   Interactions with other people help form and sustain our personal identities. As we develop from childhood to adulthood, the spoken messages we receive from our family, peers, and teachers mold our sense of who we are and how we think about ourselves. Something said by a family member or friend can serve for many years as the baseline by which we judge ourselves. A supportive word from someone we value encourages and sustains us long after we no longer see that person. At the same time, a negative evaluation or comment can affect us long after the event. The communication we receive from others contributes to the shaping of both our self-concept (how we see ourselves) and self-esteem (how we value ourselves).

3. *Social needs*
   Communication is the key to managing the dynamics of social relationships. Our choice of words affects how emotionally close or far away we are from someone. Our level of warmth or coldness can facilitate rapport or keep us strangers. Words regulate our friendships

and influence our ability to collaborate as colleagues. Adler, Rosenfeld and Towne (1995) describe six ways our social needs are met through communication:

- Pleasure–it's fun to talk to others, to laugh or otherwise interact together
- Affection–we want others to know we care, as well as hearing that we are cared for
- Inclusion–we like to belong to a group or be included in activities
- Escape–we may talk to others rather than do or think about unpleasant tasks
- Relaxation–communicating allows us to relieve tension and unwind
- Control–we attempt to influence the people or events around us.

4. *Practical needs*
   Our ability to speak clearly and in an organized manner enables us to accomplish a variety of daily tasks. When communication is not effective, we create problems that we usually label as nuisances, although they can also be more serious. For example,

   - You ask the hair stylist to take "just a little bit off the top," but the stylist cuts off too much. She interpreted your vague phrase "a little bit" to mean more than you actually had in mind. Although you may blame the stylist, your unclear instructions were a large part of the problem.
   - You tell your colleague, "I'll be back in a little while." When you return an hour later you're greeted with, "Where have you been? I've been looking for you!" As with the stylist, your colleague's interpretation of "a little" differed from your intent.
   - You call your loan company about a problem. As you complain about the poor service, the representative turns from friendly to obnoxious, and finally you feel compelled to ask for the supervisor. Your choice of words did not move you closer to the goal you had in mind before you called.

Levels of communication

Human communication involves several different levels that occur sometimes in isolation, and sometimes simultaneously.

Levels of Communication According to Number of People

Intrapersonal (Talk to ourselves)	Our thoughts and self-talk as well as occasionally speaking to ourselves out loud
Interpersonal (Talk to others)	Putting what we think and mean into words that will be interpreted by an other. We may be misunderstood be cause others don't share our history and assumptions behind the words
Group (Speak in the presence of many)	We must make ourselves clear to many different people who bring their own assumptions and understandings to our words

---

The greater the number of people, the more difficult it becomes to achieve common understandings. For example, we often accuse political candidates of providing little substance in their speeches, but they are often attempting to use common symbols which all of their audience understand and support. The number of people can also influence skills. A person who feels confident as a one-to-one communicator may feel totally inadequate in a group setting. Of course, all of the communication levels usually overlap during our interactions. Notice the levels of communication that take place in this example.

As Arthur sits at his desk, he begins planning his day. However, he has difficulty focusing because he is thinking about last night's fight with his wife. When his co-worker, Sally ,arrives with her cheerful "Good morning," he barely notices her. When he looks up and grunts, "Oh yeah, hi," Sally continues, "Arthur, what do you think of the memo on restructuring? Will it affect our division's project team? I think the changes will be great."

Arthur briefly glances up as he comments, "It's hard to know what they're up to next." Sally notices Arthur's slouched back. She says, "You look pretty down today. Anything I can do?" Arthur hesitates. "Well, I may need to take Wednesday off to deal with some things at home." Sally scans her calendar and suggests, "I can cover the project update meeting if that would help."

Arthur stands up and reaches for his briefcase. "Thanks, that would be great. Guess we better head over to the sales presentation." As Sally and Arthur walk down the hall, another colleague, Mark joins them. On their way to the meeting, they discuss events of the past week and the potential for department restructuring.

Initially, as Arthur is lost in thought about the previous night's events, he is engaging in *intra*personal communication. This communication level occurs anytime we talk to ourselves, be it silently or out loud. As Arthur and Sally exchange verbal messages, *inter*personal communication takes place. When Mark joins them on the way to the office, they begin small group communication. Clearly the possibilities for miscommunication are many. For example, if Sally were not sensitive to Arthur's mood, she might conclude that he doesn't want to be bothered with her or doesn't like her. Arthur's non-affirming style sends messages about his feelings toward Sally and her opinions. Much of his message may be unintentional, but his detachment from the conversation has negative effects just the same. Arthur's preoccupation with his home life demonstrates how our *intra*personal messages influence and are influenced by the *inter*personal messages we exchange with others. While we can artificially segregate the different types of communication, there are no distinct and exclusive categories. Most of the time we participate in several levels of communication simultaneously.

Communicating on Several Levels	
Intrapersonal + Interpersonal	My mind rehearses and prepares messages while I am speaking to a friend.
Interpersonal + Group	When I contribute to a group in a staff meeting, I also interacting with individuals in the group.
Public speaking + Interpersonal	When I speak before a large audience, I will relate nonverbally (and at times verbally) to the front row listeners who maintain eye contact and act interested.

What is interpersonal communication?

Within an organization, interpersonal communication is the process in which organizational members exchange messages for the purpose of creating shared meaning and understanding. This in turn helps accomplish organizational goals and maintain productive work relationships.

However, all communication is contextual, changing according to the setting. When we are with our families, we will say things in a different manner than when we sit in a business meeting. When we speak to colleagues, we use inferences and vernacular that an outsider would miss. Our personal history and background will shape how we say things, and the listener's history will shape how our words are heard.

The communication continuum

The context of communication shapes both the content of a message and how the message is delivered. The levels of communication form a continuum that ranges from things we say inside ourselves (even while we are speaking) to things we write or say to large audiences, mass communication.

Communication Continuum					
Intra... Personal	Inter... Personal	Small... Group	Large... Group	Public... Speaking	Mass... Communication

Along the continuum, each of the levels of communication will also be influenced by a wide range of factors. For example, interpersonal communication allows for more specific, informal contact, with immediate, spontaneous feedback. When we are speaking with a team or a large group, communication involves more formal, restricted modes and requires more planning and generalizations. The following chart (adapted from Trenholm, 1986) demonstrates how other characteristics of communication change depending on the number of people involved. Notice how each level has wide variations and how this can affect communication outcomes.

Characteristics	Interpersonal communication	Group communication
Number of people	Few	Many
Physical proximity	Close	Far
Sensory Channels	Many	Few
Nature of feedback	Immediate	Delayed
Timing of message	Informal, varied	Formal, restricted
Communication roles	Spontaneous	Planned
Message composition	Specific	General
Message adaptation	Specific	General
Goals/purpose	Relationship	Task
Levels of rules, data	Psychological, idiosyncratic	Sociological/cultural

Let's take a closer look at each of these characteristics and their effect on interpersonal communication.

- *Number of people*
  The number of people is usually two; however, small groups or teams may also include a great deal of interpersonal communication among members. Because the dynamics of group communication are more complex, some people don't communicate well in groups. The ability to listen to one person differs from listening to three or four at once. Having several people giving feedback that disagrees with our opinion can be threatening to our ego. Group dynamics are less predictable than one-to-one dynamics and for people who place a high value on control, this unpredictability can be unsettling.
- *Physical proximity of the interactants*
  Communication is typically face-to-face, at least in the early stages of relationships. But as organizational relationships progress, a greater share of interaction occurs over the phone or through e-mail. With the development of new technologies such as electronic mail and teleconferencing, people are stretching the physical distance over which they maintain interpersonal relationships. This change has created new challenges for workers more familiar with face-to-face interaction.

Recently a worker said, "In the past, distance meant talking on the phone with staff members across the city. Now I'm never sure what state or even country they're in."

It's difficult to maintain relationships when colleagues are in different buildings or even in different states. Often, even though co-workers have access to all kinds of telecommunications, they still feel a need to "do lunch" every once in a while. On the other hand, many people also complain about the cubicle office environments in which they work. Maintaining relationships can be just as difficult when there is a lack of privacy or there is constant noise, such as settings that have many workers in the same room. Closer proximity of an office may be a source of pride if it's near people of status or next to the colleagues we relate to best.

- *Sensory channels*
Closely associated with the physical presence of the communicators is the number of sensory channels available during the interaction. When both people can see, hear, touch, or smell one another, there is greater ability to correctly interpret the meaning of the message. We may be more patient with the words of a colleague who looks tired, for example, while his identical words in an e-mail message might anger us. If we see confusion on the face of our listener, we may repeat or clarify our message; when we send the same words in a fax, we are probably unaware of the confusion we cause for the receiver. Our sensory channels can add a wealth of information that helps clarify messages.

- *Nature of feedback*
When we are in each other's presence, we can usually give and receive feedback immediately. Facial expressions and voice tone also add to the information, making it richer and more comprehensive. In organizational settings, interpersonal communication generally receives immediate feedback, although sometimes the response is delayed by the use of written messages or voice-mail. Openness to *all* feedback is generally a strength of an effective communicator, but if we filter out feedback that doesn't fit our expectations or ideals, we close ourselves to valuable sources of information. A female worker commented about her relationship with a male colleague, "I can't communicate with him. What he says with his stance, his arms, and tone of voice speaks louder than his words. He complains that other females don't accept him but he won't listen to me if I try to tell him that his nonverbal messages are devaluing."

- *Timing of a message*
The timing of a message often has a great impact on its effectiveness. We will react to messages differently at the end of a day when we are

tired, than we might earlier when our patience and energy are stronger. Asking employees to do extra tasks immediately after they have finished a major project may seem like good timing, but the employees may react negatively if they need rest. Asking for a raise during the same week that the budget is due might make sense to us, but infuriate our supervisor. An important factor in effective communication is awareness of the best timing for difficult messages.

- *Communication roles*
  On one level, the roles that organizational members play are usually defined by the formal positions that people hold in the corporate structure. Titles and job descriptions tell us what our responsibilities are and to whom we report in the hierarchy. However, different managers may interpret their roles in different ways. In addition, sometimes we may call upon co-workers to assume responsibilities that are outside of their job descriptions, so the roles originally defined now become obscured.

- *Composition of messages*
  We rarely contemplate each utterance made during coffee breaks or serendipitous meetings in the elevator. But with close co-workers, we typically compose messages that are a mixture of spontaneous communications and more formal, intentional words. When writing official memos or reports, we tend to prepare more carefully both the content and the format of the documents.

- *Adaptation to the audience*
  Messages vary in their adaptation to the audience. A formal report must address the interests and needs of many people, while a specific conversation with a superior can take into consideration that person's particular style and perspective. As employees become familiar with the culture of the organization, they usually learn what they can say to each individual and how they can say it. Failure to adapt the message to the audience can get in the way of successful communication. For example, a physician had recently retired after many years as a Colonel in the Army. Now working in civilian hospitals, he frequently gave orders to the nurses in a firm, commanding tone during his hospital rounds. The nurses interpreted his statements as demeaning and unprofessional. One of them said, "He may have been able to get away with that in the military, but there's no place for him to talk to us in that manner here." The physician did not communicate effectively because he had not adapted his message to his new audience. In interpersonal communication we enhance our effectiveness when we learn how to adapt our message to a specific receiver, giving our words a stronger impact.

- *Goals or purpose*
  Messages may serve to achieve a variety of goals or purposes, such as
  to inform, persuade, build relationships, manage conflict, admonish,
  or instruct. The goal will shape each message a little differently. In
  addition, multiple goals may occur simultaneously. A manager may
  wish to firmly admonish a worker while at the same time maintaining
  a positive relationship. A worker may attempt to instruct a colleague
  on the best way to do a task while managing the potential for conflict
  created by a bruised ego. Consider the difference between these two
  responses:

  > Why did you do it this way? You seem to have a hard
  > time getting it right.
  > The way you did this task created some problems for me.
  > I know you're working hard on it, so let me suggest a few
  > changes that might help.

  In the second example, focusing on the task, not the worker, helps
  keep the message consistent with the original goals.

- *Level of rules and data*
  Communication in every context is guided by an elaborate set of
  culture-learned rules or implicit social conventions. For example, as
  children we learn how to talk respectfully to doctors, police officers,
  and parents, while the rules are different for conversations we have
  with friends. In Japan, communication rules are so firm that some
  people, even though they can't be seen, will actually bow to the
  person they're speaking with on the telephone. Avoiding eye contact
  is a sign of respect in some cultures, while in others it displays
  dishonesty. Some organizational cultures require very formal communication, while in others, informality is the rule. Failure to adapt
  appropriately may lead to significant problems in communication.
  For example, a new worker at a stock brokerage firm began giving her
  co-workers nicknames based on television shows. However, the other
  workers tended to be more formal, and they reacted negatively to the
  nicknames. As a result, the new worker soon became isolated, and
  shortly afterward she left the firm.
    When we first join an organization, our behaviors must be increas-
  ingly guided by the rules and norms of its culture. In addition, our
  level of knowledge affects our communication. At first, the information we have about other employees is usually very generic and
  stereotyped. However, as we spend time with various employees and
  get to know them as individuals, we develop individualized interaction rules, based on what we know about each person. For example,

after attending monthly sales meetings for a year, we may realize that the best way to open a meeting with the sales manager is to tell a joke. We also learn that the co-worker at the next desk doesn't even mutter a "good morning" without a cup of coffee in hand.

Stories, themes and slogans

The history of an organization plays a significant role in shaping attitudes and ultimately the interpersonal relationships within the organization. Stories about past accomplishments or organizational heroes provide valuable information for determining communication styles. As Schein (1985) puts it,

> *How the organization dealt with key competitors in the past, how it developed a new and exciting product, how it dealt with a valued employee, and so on, not only spell out the basic mission and specific goals (thereby reaffirming them) but also reaffirm the organization's picture of itself, as well as its own theory of how to get things done and how to handle interpersonal relationships. (p. 81)*

For example, communication scholars Ruth Smith and Eric Eisenberg (1987) found that during the 1970s, Disneyland was guided by the theme "the Disney family." Workers looked at fellow staff as brothers and sisters and viewed Walt Disney as the paternalistic leader. "Employees not only continued to treat the public like personal guests but came to expect similar favored treatment from management" (p. 374). Clearly an organization's guiding theme, spoken or unspoken, can have a great impact on interpersonal relationships and the effectiveness of communication that occurs in these relationships. How well an employee succeeds in a setting is in part related to his or her ability to match interpersonal behavior to the themes and slogans of the organization.

To whom am I talking?

In organizational settings, interpersonal communication involves many factors as we create and send messages to our co-workers. At times our communication resembles what we might expect between friends, and at other times it follows the formal patterns that occur in structured, more public situations. Whether we are dealing with formal or informal settings, effective communication is more likely to occur when we:

- Remain sensitive to immediate needs of others
- Build awareness of formal and informal requirements of the situation
- Choose appropriate words for the setting
- Use effective timing for what we say
- Select the best choice of words for achieving our purpose or goal
- Maintain a proper balance between portraying the role expected of us and stepping out of the role in order to address situational needs

Organizations influence how we communicate

Generally, communication involves factors over which we have control and with which we can influence outcome in relationships. We can choose the best timing, the most appropriate message for the situation, and the most effective delivery for achieving our goals. In contrast, we have far less control over dynamics created by the organizational system. Harris (1993) points out, "Organizations are systems of behavior that are interrelated and interacting rather than 'chartable' or static in nature" (p. 10). At times, we are the recipients of lack of trust elsewhere in the organization, power or control needs by some individual, or poor morale caused by a negative organizational climate.

Senge (1990) explains that understanding the dynamics of interpersonal communication in organizational settings involves:

- Recognizing interrelationships rather than linear cause-effect chains
- Acknowledging that people and events are always in a state of change (p.73).

An effective communicator develops awareness about how much the organization's system affects the communication among the workers. For example, frustration with the decision-making process may influence how cooperative we are with colleagues. Our negative attitude then influences the willingness of others to work with us. Low morale in one department can affect the morale and communication with another department. On the other hand, "Seeing the major interrelationships underlying a problem leads to new insight into what might be done" (Senge, 1990, p. 72). Maintaining positive relationships in difficult settings may become easier when we decrease the focus on "you" and "me" and acknowledge the stress created by the system in which we both work.

An effective communicator also understands that attitudes change as situations change. Words are not fixed and permanent like cement. What I say and mean today might change tomorrow. Viewing people and events as isolated, unchanging snapshots, does not allow for the process of change constantly occurring around us. Patience, coupled with a desire for understanding, however, will create successful communicators.

Assessing a Communication Event

Write out a brief description of a recent interaction, such as a meeting or a conversation. Answer the following questions about the situation.

1. How were the following needs satisfied during the interaction?

   Physical needs

   Identity needs

   Social needs

   Practical needs

2. How many different interaction configurations occurred, i.e. one-to-one, one-to-two, and one-to-three or more?

3. What was the physical proximity of the participants?

4. What sensory channels did the individuals use?

5. Was feedback immediate or delayed?

6. How would you assess the timing of the messages?

7. What communications roles did each participant play?

8. Was the composition and adaptation of the messages specific or general ?

9. What were specific goals or purposes?

10. What rules and information guided the action?

11. Did organizational factors affect the interaction?

CHAPTER TWO

The Complex Foundation of Interpersonal Communication

Organizational challenges to communication

Interpersonal communication would be simpler if it occurred in a laboratory where the distractions were carefully controlled. But in real life, our communication is influenced by a complex blend of factors: the people involved, the setting, individual listening skills, distractions, and communication styles.

Within organizations, the process becomes even more complicated. Add layers of authority, a broad range of education backgrounds, disparity of skills and competence, high demands, and corporate expectations. Determining how to improve communication requires better understanding of the complicated elements that contribute to the communication process.

A model for understanding communication

The communication model that follows, separates the components of communication in order to better illustrate the whole picture. This model identifies the factors within organizations that influence communication, along with the theoretical concepts associated with each component and how they relate to each other.

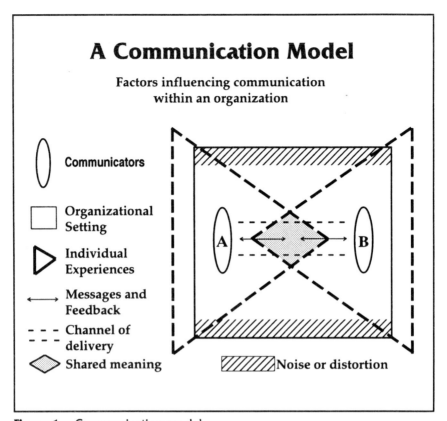

Figure 1.   Communication model

Each component occurs separately yet simultaneously, resulting in constantly changing variables that complicate the goals of effective communication.

The communicators

Notice how the people represented by the ovals A and B function as both senders and receivers of messages. At any given moment, a communicator's predominant role may switch from sender to receiver, then back again. What makes communication an interactive process is the ability to change roles instantly, along with adapting our message in response to the other participant. For example, while one person is expressing her ideas about the logistics for a new project, the other person grimaces, showing disagreement with the feasibility of the idea. The speaker may then change her message as she creates it, by modifying her idea or including justifications in order to accommodate the receiver's feedback. Although both people are sending and receiving messages at the same time, we can understand the process better if we break it down into two parts: encoding and decoding (Verderber & Verderber, 1995).

How we code messages

Encoding	When a communicator sends a message. This is a cognitive process that transforms ideas or feeling into symbols and behaviors, then organizes them into a message.
Decoding	When a communicator receives a message. Translating the verbal and nonverbal symbols or behaviors into the receiver's own feelings or ideas.

These processes happen so fast that we usually don't even think about them. Only when we are having difficulty finding the right words, or figuring out the meaning of a confusing message, do we slow down the processes and bring them to a conscious level. For example, if your manager sees problems with your strategy for a new marketing plan, she may hesitate slightly, searching for a way to encode a message that tells you that she doesn't think it will work. She may say something like, "That's interesting." When you hear this message, you may recall synonyms for "interesting," such as *fascinating, attractive* or even *exciting*. But you probably know from previous conversations that "interesting" is a way of telling you that she wants to reject your plan without hurting your feelings.

In organizations, we must remember that any person who is capable of picking up the message and decoding it can become a receiver. It might be the person for whom the message was intended, or someone who simply has access to receiving the message. As our technology expands, the chances for unintended receivers to pick up messages are drastically increased, either through carelessness or through misuse of the technology. For example, have you ever forgotten to remove your original from the copier or fax machine because you were in a hurry to get to a meeting? Has someone forwarded your voice-mail or e-mail messages to another employee without your permission? As message senders, we need to consider who might be a receiver besides the person for whom the message was intended.

The organizational setting

The solid rectangle in the model depicts the organizational setting. Our work environment impacts how we conduct ourselves in general, as well as how we communicate with each other specifically. Organizational setting includes things such as the physical surroundings, the expected degree of formality in talk, dress and behavior codes, the written and the implied rules, the nature of the relationships between employees, and the organizational climate. The components of the organizational setting provide a framework and set constraints on the ways that the communicators interact. Even the organization's history, image, and expectations for performance serve as guidelines for acceptable and unacceptable ways of acting and ultimately affect the communication process.

Individual experiences

The heavy dashed triangles in the model show the influence of each communicator's individual differences. Notice how the triangles extend beyond the organizational-setting rectangle, indicating that people's relevant experiences include more than their lives at work. Long before joining a specific corporation, individuals have developed attitudes, expectations and self-concepts. Families and communities, ethnic, racial or social cultures, and experiences in other organizations, all color our communication patterns. Through their social contacts, workers accumulate personal histories and memories, attitudes toward other people and events, and expectations about themselves in general, including their performance in the work place. Individual's self-concept powerfully guides and influences behaviors and communication with other employees.

Messages and feedback

Typically the initial information sent is designated as the message, while the response is referred to as feedback. However, this is an arbitrary designation, since we are constantly sending and receiving messages. The way we punctuate the interaction determines which information serves as the initiating behavior and which is the response. For example, Lisa knocks softly on the open door to Walter's office and quietly asks, "Are you ready for the meeting?" Walter, intensely poring over the stack of reports on his desk, answers gruffly, "Come in!" When Lisa initially looked into his office, Walter's nonverbal message was that he was engrossed in his paperwork and did not want to be interrupted. She tried to be as non-intrusive as possible in her feedback to his body language. However, Walter interpreted Lisa's behavior as so unassertive that he had to respond with some kind of command to get her to enter the room.

We are usually involved in continuous streams of behavior in which each message serves as the feedback for the previous message. Whatever we identify as the beginning of the interaction determines what is considered the first message and what is labeled as feedback. In Walter's mind, the interaction began when Lisa knocked. By identifying Lisa as the initiator, he perceived his responses as feedback. From Lisa's viewpoint, Walter's nonverbal behavior started the interaction. Her feedback was to be quiet and unobtrusive and to communicate that she respected his space.

In organizational communication, the term *feedback* is also used to refer to some response to an employee's level of performance. Research has shown that performance improves with positive feedback and decreases with negative feedback (Kohli & Jaworski, 1994). Additionally, the fairly new concept of 360-degree feedback, in which each employee rates every other employee, is being explored as a tool which organizations could use not only for evaluation, but also for developing and maintaining the company's competitive edge in the marketplace (London & Beatty, 1993).

The type of message used will also influence the communication outcome. Any information transmitted by voice is termed a vocal message. However not all vocal messages are verbal, involving linguistic symbols or words. Sighs, groans, humming, and sobbing all give vocal messages without using words.

Nonvocal messages range from written verbal communications to observations that we assign meanings to, such as apparel or the furnishings in an office. Both vocal and nonvocal messages can communicate a different meaning than we intended, sometimes at an unconscious level. "Freudian slips," or the unintentional uttering of a curse word may result in a very different message than what was planned by the speaker.

Finally, messages are altered by the cues surrounding the actual words. Voice inflections, gestures, posture, facial expression, even clothing and furniture all affect the way a message is received and interpreted. Watzlawick, Bavelas and Jackson (1967) refer to this as the *report* and *command* aspects of a message. If your colleague, using a light, melodic voice, says, "Hey, how are you doing with that report?" You may interpret the question as a supportive message. If the question is asked in a harsh and deliberate tone, you may perceive it as a warning.

Channel of delivery

The channel of delivery contributes additional information to our messages when we interact. In general, the five senses serve as channels to transmit messages: hearing, sight, touch, smell and taste. In face-to-face communication, we hear the person's words and note the rate of speech, the quality of the vocal tone and the loudness of the voice. We watch the individual's gestures and posture, eye contact, and the physical surroundings. We may notice that he or she has a strong handshake and even comment on the faint air of a fragrance. By far, this face-to-face interaction is the richest in available information because it utilizes the most channels.

The nature of work in organizations frequently requires communicating with people who are not physically present, so we substitute telephones, voice-mail and e-mail as the channel (Johnson, 1992). We capture messages in letters, memos, and reports and send them via fax. With the advent of new technologies, such as videotext, teleconferencing, and interactive computing, we can combine technical channels with approximations of face-to-face experiences.

Researchers studying electronic communication channels have looked at how they compare to face-to-face interactions. Ugbah and Dewine (1989) found that the new technologies tend to be used more for task-related communication than for relational communication. Managers reported that the technologies improved the perceived organizational climate and the provision of adequate information. Ugbah and Devine also noted that, when employees made conscious efforts to maintain interpersonal relationships, electronic technologies did not create problems. Other studies have found mixed or negative effects. McLeod (1992) analyzed 13 studies that focused on the use of electronic systems by groups and various group processes. These studies concluded that groups using electronic support for decision making had arrived at higher quality decisions, focused more on the task, and experienced a greater equality in participation in decisions. However, these groups also took more time to reach decisions, had less consensus about the decisions, and experienced less satisfaction with the process.

Another study compared the difference between video-conferencing and face-to-face meetings (O'Conaill, Whittaker & Wilbur, 1993). Video-conferencing resulted in a more formal conversation style and less communication response, such as people saying "uh-huh" or nodding to encourage the speaker to continue. Transmission lags also affected the interactions. While people interrupted each other less, they also had difficulty anticipating when another person was finished speaking.

The most productive and satisfying work environments generally use modern technologies in conjunction with face-to-face interactions, supplying the maximum flow of information as well as retaining opportunities to interact with fellow workers. In 1995, a reporter from *U. S. News & World Report* visited the offices of entrepreneur Michael Bloomberg on Park Avenue in New York (Haas, 1995). Bloomberg's $650 million media empire is housed on floors 11 through 17 of a high-rise building. However, the office arrangement is unique in that the elevator stops only on the 14th floor, forcing the employees to move from floor to floor on a narrow spiral staircase that connects the seven floors. The company also offers a free full-service cafeteria. Bloomberg's strategy is a simple one: create opportunities for face-to-face interaction that generates information-sharing, which leads to creativity and better media coverage. The more employees "bump into each other" and share meals together, the more productive they will be.

Noise

Anything that distorts or affects the accuracy or clarity of the message, the efficiency of transmission, or the meaning intended, constitutes noise. Three types of noise can interfere with creating, sending or receiving messages: physical, physiological, or psychological noise (Adler & Rodman, 1994).

Physical noise describes factors in the environment that make it difficult for either person to attend to the interaction. For example, if you are in a meeting and the room is uncomfortably warm, the projection screen is too far away to see, or you can't hear the speaker because of the loud air-conditioning system, you are experiencing physical noise.

Physiological noise refers to biological factors inside the communicators that impair the ability to create or decipher messages. Have you ever said, "I'm so tired, I can't put two words together"? Or have you ever tried to finish a project while fighting a cold or the flu? Fatigue, hunger, illness, pain, even excitement, can all result in physiological noise.

Finally, psychological noise occurs when individual experiences interfere with effective communication. Cultural background and native language may put a listener at a disadvantage when trying to understand American slang. Or the use of sexist language or an unacceptable label may infuriate a receiver to the point where he or she no longer listens to the message. When you are anxious and worried about the report you must finish by 5:00 p.m. today, and you can't concentrate on the vice president's update speech, you are experiencing psychological noise.

Shared meaning

Bringing all the elements of the communication model together shows that effective communication is a complex process. Successfully encoding and decoding messages, selecting the appropriate channel or channels for transmission, and eliminating distracting noise improve communication but may not be sufficient. Shared meaning results when organizational and individual experiences overlap because of commonalties in backgrounds, cultures, training, or life experiences. When this happens, both people understand the message in primarily the same way, and their interpretations of the message will be similar. When people come from synchronous backgrounds and have similar perceptions of their environment, it becomes easier for them to arrive at shared meanings. The converse is also true: The more disparate their life experiences, cultures, or work environments, the harder it will be to arrive at a common understanding of the messages they exchange. With the changing demographics of the work force and the move-ment toward international business, workers need to take into account how different cultural and historical backgrounds affect communication (Kikoski, 1993). We must realize that our own culture and history, as well as that of the other person, influence all aspects of the communication process.

Purpose of the model

The communication model helps us dissect the way messages are given and received, along with recognizing the myriad of variables that affect the outcome. The communicators themselves bring a range of individual experiences to the setting in which communication takes place. As they send messages and receive feedback, they attempt to choose the ap-propriate channel of delivery, and to minimize distortion of the mes-sage from noise and distractions. When the factors overlap effectively, the communicators experience shared meaning, a mutual understand-ing of what was communicated between them.

Application of the Communication Model

1. Recall two recent encounters with co-workers, one that you considered successful and one that you evaluated as unsuccessful. Using the components of the communication model describe what contributed to the outcome in each situation. Did some factors impact the outcome more than others? If so, which ones and why? What could you do differently to change the outcome of the unsuccessful interaction?

2. Give an example of how each component of the communication model has affected an interpersonal communication experience that you've had at work. Did the factors positively or negatively influence the interaction?

CHAPTER THREE

Factors that Shape the Communication Message

"What we have here is a failure to communicate."
Paul Newman, *Cool Hand Luke*

In our efforts to be effective communicators, we frequently encounter obstacles that make the process difficult. We may send nonverbal messages that contradict our spoken words. Our listener may filter out parts of our message, altering our intended meaning. To become more effective, we need to recognize and understand how those factors influence the communication outcome.

Perception

We are constantly receiving many stimuli from the world and people around us. If we took in every bit of information that comes at us, we would suffer from continuous information overload. So we notice and attend to some of these stimuli and overlook others. At a party we might engage in an intense conversation while surrounded by other people talking, as well as background music. Our perceptions allow us to make sense of the things we experience and use that understanding to function effectively. As we assign meaning to our experiences, we go through three stages in the perception process: selection, organization, and interpretation (Adler, Rosenfeld & Towne, 1995).

29

Stage 1: Selection

Since we cannot pay attention to every stimulus or message we are ex-posed to, we select which information we will attend to and which we will ignore. These choices in selection are guided by our physical sensory capabilities and by psychological factors of interest, need, and expecta-tion (Verderber & Verderber, 1995).

Our sensory capabilities often determine what portion of the physical world we can access. For example, some people have difficulty hearing conversations in a noisy restaurant. We also attend more to information that interests us. Individuals who are fascinated with computers will av-idly read every computer magazine available, while computer-phobics don't even see them on the supermarket shelf.

Similarly, if we have a need to know the information, we will pay close attention to related stimuli. For instance, if the discussion in a budget meet-ing impacts the operation of our department, we will remember virtually everything that was said, while if the topic does not affect us directly, we may tune out much of the conversation. We also tend to focus on stimuli we expect to occur and frequently fail to pick up on unexpected stimuli. If a co-worker routinely delivers reports late, we may not notice the one time his report comes in early. This first stage of perception serves as an initial screen or filter, so we can monitor and control information to keep it manageable.

Stage 2: Organization

Information is sent to the brain void of any logical sequence or order. If we simply stored data as it came in, we would have a hard time finding it or using it. So the brain sorts and organizes the information using catego-ries similar to the those we might develop to file papers or shelve books in a library. We typically organize things by functional relationships, simi-larity of topics, chronology, or word rhythms. With respect to people, we tend to classify them according to physical appearance, social roles or be-haviors, and psychological characteristics (Andersen, 1993). Sometimes we create "standard packages" of descriptors for people that lead to ste-reotypes. While this categorization system may be helpful as a type of shorthand, we might base our reactions to people on misperceptions in-stead of how the people really are.

Stage 3: Interpretation

The final stage in the perception process involves making sense out of the information. Since messages can have a variety of meanings, we need to consolidate what we know about the person, the situation, and the actual words in order to figure out the meaning of the interaction. Suppose you deliver your proposal for a new marketing plan, and both Marty and Janice frown during your presentation. You know from your past experiences that Marty's frown means he is trying to follow your rationale, while Janice's frown probably means she will not approve it.

Perception depends on each person's experiences as well as the organizational setting in which the interactions take place. It influences how communicators structure and respond to messages. Perception is easily altered by "noise" that may distort or block the transmission of the message.

Listening and how it works

Listening and hearing are not always the same. A person may look at us intently, hear our words, but have no idea what we are saying because he isn't listening. Hearing is the physiological process that begins when the outer ear gathers sound waves from the environment and translates the subsequent vibrations into impulses which are carried to the brain. This physiological process occurs outside of our control. Even when we are sleeping we receive messages because we are still hearing.

Listening is a broader process which includes the three stages of perception along with the interaction-based steps of remembering and responding (Adler, Rosenfeld & Towne, 1995). Our ability to remember information decreases rapidly with the passage of time. Immediately after hearing something, we may remember only half of the information. After eight hours this drops to 35%, and two months later we will have lost 10% more of what we heard (Wolvine & Coakley, 1993).

What and how much we remember is also determined by how we store the data. Our memory is composed of three kinds of storage: the sensory register, short-term memory and long-term memory. The sensory register can hold a great deal of information for a short period of time. For example, we might be introduced to people and remember their names during a meeting, but forget them as soon as we leave the room. We can recall a telephone number long enough to dial it but have to look it up again if the line is busy. Unless the information put in the sensory register is selected and attended to quickly, it will be lost.

Short-term memory conducts conscious and active mental processes on the information and holds it on a temporary basis. Our short-term memory has a limited capacity and can quickly be overloaded, especially if we are stressed or very busy. For example, when we park our car at the mall, we can usually walk right to it when we are done shopping. However, sometimes, such as at the holidays, we may not be able to remember where we parked because we are overloaded with other short-term memory requirements. If we process information extensively, by using the organization and understanding stages of perception, we can store it in long-term memory. This memory component has infinite capacity and holds everything that we have previously experienced.

Types of listening

Listening takes place within a person. The next step is responding to the message and giving feedback. We have more control over this aspect of the process. Depending on the type of feedback we give, we will engage in one of three kinds of listening:

- Passive listening
- Directive responses
- Active listening

Passive listening involves paying attention, but not offering any verbal feedback. We do this anytime we sit in a meeting but don't offer any comments as we listen.

A second kind of listening, directive responses, usually does one of the following: supports the speaker through agreement, offers an interpretation of the message and justifies why, passes judgment, or offers advice by evaluating the speaker's ideas and behaviors.

Active listening involves paying attention and reflecting on the message rather than providing direction (Adler, Rosenfeld & Towne, 1995). You verify that your perception of the message was accurate and that you understand not only the speaker's ideas, but also the feelings behind the words. Active listening utilizes a variety of responses. Paraphrasing or restating the speaker's message in your own words, lets the person know how you interpreted the message. You might verbalize your sense of the speaker's feelings associated with the message, giving him or her the opportunity to confirm or correct your understanding of the message.

Active listening uses a combination of open-ended and closed-ended questions as a tool for digging deeper into a subject. At times it is useful to ask specific closed-ended questions such as, "Do you want this project completed by Friday?" or "In which format do you want the final report?" Failing to ask for specific instructions is often a source of miscommunication in organizations. Open-ended questions are useful for creating a non-confrontive, non-argumentative atmosphere in which others can tell us more about what they think and feel, such as, "I notice that this report is late. Were there some things that got in the way?" or "We're just not getting this completed properly. Have you got some ideas on how we can get this right?" The goal is understanding without creating defensiveness.

Active listening also involves empathizing, or being sensitive to the feelings behind the communication. Acknowledging the other person's thoughts and feelings doesn't mean that you agree with his or her ideas and emotions. Empathy simply serves as a way to validate the thoughts and feelings of others in a way that builds trust and honesty in the relationship.

For most people, active listening is not something we do naturally, but it is a skill that can be learned. It requires that we focus our attention on the words of others, communicate that we are genuinely interested in what they have to say, and demonstrate openness to what we hear, even if it disagrees with how we see things.

Language is an arbitrary system of symbols

Language is the system of symbols that we use to construct messages, which in turn enables us to create shared meanings and regulate relationships. Language consists of groupings of symbols that in themselves have no meaning. We combine symbols to create words, then arbitrarily assign these symbols to represent objects or ideas. For example, the word "desk" refers to a piece of office furniture, but in no way resembles that object. We associate the symbol with the object because we generally agree on the meaning. The ability to verbalize our thoughts allows us to conceptualize objects and ideas that are far beyond the observable world we live in. The effectiveness of language depends on our ability to make our messages clear and unambiguous. When we develop awareness about the rules that make messages more appropriate than others, and manage the relative and abstract terms, we construct more appropriate messages based on shared frames of reference. To reduce misunderstandings in our communication we must be aware that we use symbols that must constantly be explained and clarified. We also create new symbols when we need them. With advances in technology, we have created words that didn't exist fifty years ago, such as *polyester* and *fax* (Adler & Rodman, 1994; Adler, Rosenfeld & Towne, 1995; Tubbs & Moss, 1994).

Some words require an understanding of the context if we are to understand their meaning fully. A friend recently arranged to meet her shopping partner at the front door of a department store. After waiting for twenty minutes, she realized that her friend was at the "front door" at another store entrance. Cultural differences may also result in some words being familiar to the user but not to the receiver. As business interactions become more global, we may encounter words that require more explanation to arrive at shared meaning.

Language is governed by rules

To insure that people use the arbitrary symbols in the same way, language has rules that tell us how to create and use the symbols. Two common types include syntactic and semantic rules.

Syntactic rules determine the structure of the language. They tell us how to combine letters to make words and how to arrange words in sentences. For example, words in English never contain strings of consonants such as "czyn," although words in other languages do. Similarly, we would be puzzled if we heard, "Are you to the meeting coming?" asked by an English-speaking co-worker, but not if the words came from a colleague speaking German.

Semantic rules determine the meaning of the words depending on the context in which they are used. We use these rules to judge the exact meaning of the message and the intentions of the speaker. For example, the statement, "Let's get together later this week," has different meanings when said by a friend than by a supervisor.

An effective communicator develops a high level of sensitivity to the rules for using appropriate language in a variety of settings. Using perfectly correct sentence structure may in some settings give the impression of superiority and aloofness, while at other times may be required for the situation. In some areas women may feel esteemed and youthful when referred to as a "girl" but in other settings this would be viewed as a sign of sexism or disrespect. Inappropriate use of language may create laughter in some settings, but in others it may cause perceptions of insensitivity or verbal abuse.

Language possesses a high degree of relativity

Relative terms rely on the creator's frame of reference and depend heavily on others sharing a similar frame of reference. An engineering staff is directed to, "design a new product that is cheaper and of higher quality than the competition's." The staff members must now determine the meaning of *cheaper* and *quality*, which are relative terms even within their own company.

The performance appraisal process becomes difficult when managers and employees lack agreement on the use of words, such as *good* or *adequate*. Morale is often linked to employee ratings based on a point scale. Even though the points have specific descriptions, the descriptions may appear relative to the evaluator's frame of reference. The inherent property of language's relativity means that every word and phrase is only an approximation of what we mean. Effective communicators must be on guard against differing frames of reference in order to maintain clarity and shared meaning.

Language varies in level of abstraction

The more vague the description of the event or object, the more difficult it is to arrive at an accurate interpretation of the message (Hayakawa, 1964). For example, a company vice president told his facilities manager to move a department of 30 personnel out of a particular area and to redesign the area with better utilization of space. He said, "I want the managers more accessible to the workers and the area rearranged for better work flow." A month later the facility director presented the vice president with three alternatives for the area's design. They included a cost analysis and time chart to estimate completion of the project. The vice president was indignant. "I didn't ask you for three proposals. I told you what I wanted and how I wanted it. I want those desks moved around to improve the efficiency of the work area. Now go do it!"

This vice president had in the past expected detailed analysis for similar types of projects. He tended to alternate in his communication style between quite vague and very specific. The facilities manager had to try to guess what level of abstraction the vice president was using and determine whether to generate an extensive plan or simply move desks.

Language allows for the creation of the negative

The symbolic nature of spoken language enables us to identify both things that are, and things that are not. Thoughts and ideas can create symbolic representations of possibilities not yet realized, and of problems that might emerge given the right set of circumstances. We can infer, anticipate and speculate. We can discuss war at the same time we talk of peace. Events of the past can influence thoughts in the present and alter plans for the future. Without language, there would be no way to tell your staff that you will *not* be at the meeting tomorrow morning. Without language, when they arrive at the meeting, all they can understand is who *is* there.

Language's ability to allow us to anticipate what the future will be or speculate about the outcome of decisions has been a significant driving force in human progress. The downside is that for every positive there is a negative, and for every possibility there is an impossibility. You want to plan a picnic for next month but discussion bogs down when someone worries about the possibility of rain. Your proposal for a new product is greeted by discussion of possible downturns in the market. Language's very nature creates pessimism to live along side of optimism.

The implication for this aspect of language is that statements negative or opposite to our point of view should not automatically be rejected.

Instead, they should be the focus of dialogue. Never kill the question; focus the dialogue on it. If creation of the negative is inherent in communication, then we should learn to live with it and channel its power.

Communication climate

Ramie Becker, marketing communication manager for the Colorado Lottery, works with many different organizations, both public and private. She describes great differences in the work environments. Some are cold and formal, without much social interaction. In these corporations people are protective of ideas and highly loyal to their departments. But she also sees organizations where the style is warm, casual, and more personal than businesslike. Here she observes more dialogue and a greater spirit of equality.

Becker is not referring to the products or services of the organizations but the communication climate that is evident almost immediately. Whether warm, cold, formal, casual, accepting, or rigid, the organizational climate affects everything from daily conversations to decision-making processes. An organization's communication climate is composed of two factors:

1. Structural properties of the organization, which include the beliefs, values and expectations of the organization, typically identified by policies, procedures and rules.
2. The systems of observable behaviors, interactions and practices of employees. (Pace & Faules, 1994; Poole, 1985)

Factors that influence communication climates

Communication climates can be described and analyzed in nine dimensions: interdependence, openness, confirmation, similarity, trust, equality, equity, control, and task versus social orientation (Moorhead, 1991). The significance of each of these factors changes with the setting.

Interdependence

Interdependence refers to the degree that individuals rely on each other to do their jobs and accomplish their goals. Coule (1993) notes that some interdependence is necessary to allow employees to grow and adapt to the changing environment. This interdependent growth directly impacts the productivity of an organization.

An organization functions as a system when group members rely on the cooperation and input of others in order to get work completed. Computer programmers may work independently in a work station, but they depend on accurate information being sent to them by others. Sales staff may do their calls in an independent style, but they need their corporate office to supply the product, pay expenses and provide current market information. Very few jobs have complete autonomy. Interdependence is achieved in a healthy organizational climate by cooperation and collaboration with others. Secrecy, distrust, and turf battles may be present in an organization lacking in healthy interdependence.

Openness

An open climate is one in which people can easily share what they think and feel without fear of harm or retribution. Emotional safety, trust, and support are required to maintain an open communication climate. If during a staff meeting, a long-time employee responds to a new employee by saying, "That was a dumb question," the climate will feel unsafe and the new employee will withhold comments at future meetings. A colleague once said, "It's predictable. Every time I speak up in our meetings, the associate manager will disagree with what I say. I'd like to contribute more, but I'm fearful that the group will side with him and discredit my ideas."

Openness is especially critical when corporations undergo mergers and acquisitions (Bastien, 1987). Accurate and complete information can help employees deal with their high levels of uncertainty about their positions in the redefined organization.

The degree of openness that organizational members experience affects their ability to make decisions and set policies. The members of top management who set the course for the organization must be able to discuss sensitive issues openly in order to make decisions that support a shared vision (Alderson, 1993). Openness also includes sharing information so that appropriate organizational policies can be formulated (Johnsson, 1992). Newman (1990) reports that Polaroid Corporation effectively dealt with information filtering by changing the format of its weekly informational meetings and expanding participation to include all salaried employees.

Jerry Johnson, former senior vice president at US West Communications, says, "We do not have a long history of frank 'give and take' discussions. Key technology decisions traditionally have been made behind closed doors, without holding them up to the test of intellectual rigor and a clear understanding of the pros and cons. We need to eliminate *group think* and create a spirit of interaction in our culture" (Spangle & Knapp, 1996).

An open climate encourages points of view that may not agree with our own. Badawy (1994) found that successful teams display a greater willingness to engage in contributing criticism about decisions and ideas. Closed organizational climates inhibit innovation and restrict the ability of the group to adapt effectively to change.

Confirmation

Confirmation is a term that describes our perceptions about how we are valued. Most people will work harder and express a greater willingness to cooperate when they believe their ideas are being heard and their skills appreciated. People feel disconfirmed when they believe that they are not listened to or that their opinions are not valued.

Sieburg (1985) says that confirming behaviors take place at three levels; recognition, acknowledgment, and endorsement. Recognition involves an awareness of another person's presence and a willingness to relate. We acknowledge the presence of others through smile, a handshake, or a "glad you're here." Acknowledgment creates a climate in which people demonstrate greater willingness to interact. Employees will engage in conversation more easily with those who acknowledge the importance of their presence.

The highest level of confirmation, endorsement, involves affirming the validity of another person's experiences. Endorsement does not mean that we must agree with the person; we affirm that the person has a right to his or her viewpoint.

A well-known admiral recently visited a Navy base and was invited to eat lunch in the cafeteria. Generally officers do not interact with enlisted personnel in military settings. But as the admiral moved through the cafeteria line, he suddenly stopped, turned, and walked behind the dividing partition to where the cooks were working. He then shook hands with each one and told them what a good job they were doing. The cooks were amazed and smiled in appreciation of his gesture. One said, "No admiral has even noticed me before, and now one shook my hand!" The admiral recognized their presence as well as acknowledging their importance.

Organizations can demonstrate confirmation of employees in a number of ways. Management confirms the contribution of workers by designing rewards that provide recognition of high-caliber teamwork, including monetary bonuses, greater visibility in the company, promotions, access to senior management and corporate awards (Badawy, 1994). Braham (1993) suggests that workers can be affirmed publicly through a congratulatory letter, a choice of work assignments, flex-time, a new title, additional training of their choice, or time off.

The most practical form of confirmation occurs when daily we acknowledge the worth of our co-workers, communicate appreciation for the little things that few notice, and validate the importance of their opinions, regardless of their status in the organization.

Similarity

We are attracted to people with similar beliefs, values, attitudes, interests and personal characteristics. This attraction occurs for many reasons. We find common themes to discuss, such as the latest sporting event or the weather. We can predict people's responses because they think or act similarly to the way we do. People who share common beliefs make us feel more confident and less alone, thereby validating our self-concept. With people who are similar to us, such as sharing our sense of humor, we feel more freedom to be ourselves.

Similarity weighs heavily on our judgments about the nature of an organizational climate. If co-workers are too dissimilar, we may judge the climate to be cold, distant and unaccepting. On the other hand, if everyone values many of the things we do, we may perceive the climate as friendly, warm, and comfortable. This factor explains why two people who share similar education and skills can have vastly different experiences in the same work group. To have happy and effective workers, managers should try to fashion work groups with sufficient similarities to promote friendships, yet enough differences to encourage creativity.

Trust

Because so much of organizational climate depends on cooperation and sharing of information, trust is a major component. Trust requires a perception of emotional or physical safety with people equally committed to the best interests of the others.

Trust means different things to different people. When asked how they know they can trust someone, some people say, "I can expect that he will do what he says he'll do." Other people describe trust as their ability to be vulnerable without being betrayed. Many people associate trust with a person's credibility and integrity. In a study of middle managers by Schindler and Thomas (1993), trust was defined as including competence, consistency, integrity, loyalty, and openness. Whether the managers were addressing their relationships with superiors, peers, or subordinates, the most important aspects of trust were integrity, competence and loyalty.

Equality

The dimension of equality refers to a communication climate in which individuals treat each other with mutual respect (Burgoon & Hale, 1987). Gibb (1961) identifies equality as an important characteristic of a supportive climate and superiority as a significant characteristic of a defensive climate. Successful managers demonstrate equality by giving fair treatment to all ideas presented in group discussions and by trying to maintain consistent standards when making decisions. Wilson, Hantz and Hanna (1995) explain that we "display equality by not *pulling rank*, minimizing differences in ability, status and power; treating the other person's view with the same respect that we give to our own views" (p. 236). We demonstrate equality in conversations when we emphasize similarities in perception or ideas before we turn to focus on differences. Equality exists in conflict management when we express value for the opinions of others. In negotiation, equality occurs as both parties acknowledge the importance of each other's interests. Communication climates that have more messages of superiority than messages of equality create an atmosphere that is less friendly, emotionally cold, and at times, even hostile. Superiority messages devalue others, demonstrate a lack of acceptance, and deflate egos. Once a defensive climate begins, it tends to spiral downward into greater and greater destructive communication patterns. In contrast, communicating respect and equality creates a climate of greater cooperation and mutual supportiveness.

Equity

Equality and equity are sometimes used interchangeably. However, they are actually two distinct dimensions of a communication climate. *Equality* refers to mutual respect, *equity* pertains to people's sense of fair treatment. Employees feel they are treated equitably when the rewards they receive from the organization are proportional to their efforts. A major problem in downsizing organizations is that there are fewer promotions and raises to reward performance. When a worker with less experience or seniority is promoted over a more qualified employee, a feeling of unfairness results.

A perception of an inequitable climate creates distrust of leadership and hurts communication patterns. At a community college in Denver, physical plant workers began criticizing each other harshly when they learned that there would be only one job promotion for the year. They described the school as having an inequitable organizational climate characterized by uncaring leaders. Criticism began to decrease when discussion began about creating a committee with employee representation that would allocate raises or promotions based on objective criteria.

Control

Control defines the nature of relationships by determining the right of one individual to decide or influence the behaviors of another person. We expect managers to have some influence over how subordinates do their jobs, but they can accomplish this in many different ways. Baker (1994) identifies several traditional methods of management that depend on excessive control:

- *Ultra-control*
  The manager plans everything in advance and makes people behave like parts of a machine by specifying tasks, activities, and jobs in excruciating detail.

- *Managing by the numbers*
  The manager sets performance targets, usually sales or profit objectives, but workers are on their own to figure out what to do to meet their targets.
- *Over-reliance on pay as a motivator*
  The manager ignores the opportunity to tap other powerful motivating forces, such as the needs for social approval, acceptance, achievement, self-esteem, and self-fulfillment. (p. 10-11)

Baker recommends the philosophy of empowerment as an alternative to controlling management techniques. Managers can increase empowerment in employees by encouraging team building and networking, providing resources and training, and encouraging flexibility and improvisation (p. 14-15).

Perceptions of empowerment versus control center on the kind of decision-making processes utilized by an organization. Parker and Price (1994) found that employees felt empowered when their managers had control over decision-making and the managers were supportive of their workers.

Sometimes different management styles are used at different levels of an organization. A study by Lamude and Scudder (1991) showed that middle-level managers were more likely to use relational messages reflecting participative decision-making than were upper-level or lower-level managers. Upper-level managers tended to use messages that were more formal or expressed dominance.

Task versus social orientation

Communication climate is also determined by the mix of focus on task versus social orientations (Burgoon et al., 1989). People who tend to be task-oriented are mainly interested in "getting the job done." They focus on setting clear goals, organizing projects by directing and controlling activities and establishing time lines. Task-oriented individuals typically like to take control of decision-making and then *tell* others what the outcome is.

Employees who focus almost exclusively on task-related goals are often labeled workaholics or Type A personalities. These individuals not only introduce stress into their own lives, but also add stress to the organizational climate because of their extremely competitive behavior patterns and idealistic standards of productivity. In Lamude, Scudder and Dickson's (1993) study of 112 primary care physicians, high Type A scores were associated with the use of more dominance, formality, and task-orientation and less similarity when these physicians communicated with patients.

People who emphasize social aspects of interactions are more concerned with maintaining high morale, including everyone in the work activity and establishing a harmonious atmosphere. They are interested in developing supportive relationships and attending to the personal lives and emotions that others bring to the work setting. Socially oriented people lean toward facilitating decision-making processes and using consensus to arrive at solutions. However, if the climate is weighted too heavily toward a social orientation, i.e. providing support, listening, facilitating interactions, and so on, the employees may become entrenched in the processes and lose track of the organization's mission and goals.

Social and task orientations are not either/or characteristics. A person may exhibit low levels of both orientations, high levels of both, or various combinations of attention to task and social aspects of the setting. People will often evaluate their work atmosphere in terms of the task and social orientations and behave accordingly. Certainly, the nature of an organization will determine the proper degrees of task and social orientations, but organizations need a balance of the two aspects in order to create and maintain a productive and supportive climate.

Assessing Your Organizational Climate

Think about a single context, such as your work group, your department, or your organization. Assess the group with the following questions.

1. To what extent does *openness* describe the communication between members of your group?

5	4	3	2	1
Completely	A great deal	Moderately	Only a little	Almost none

2. How much do rumors characterize the primary source of information in your group?

5	4	3	2	1
Almost none	A little	Moderately	A great deal	Completely

3. How often do you think constructive problem solving occurs in your group?

5	4	3	2	1
Most of the time	Often	Moderately	Occasionally	Rarely

4. How often do problems occur because of miscommunication, or non-communication, between leaders and group members?

5	4	3	2	1
Rarely	Occasionally	Moderately	Often	Most of the time

5. How often do group members communicate *support* for each other?

5	4	3	2	1
Most of the time	Often	Moderately	Occasionally	Rarely

6. How often is decision making secretive or unclear in your group?

5	4	3	2	1
Rarely	Occasionally	Moderately	Often	Most of the time

7. How often does defensiveness or someone's ego get in the way of constructive discussion in your group?

5	4	3	2	1
Rarely	Occasionally	Moderately	Often	Most of the time

8. How often do members communicate acceptance or emotionally warmth toward each other?

5	4	3	2	1
Most of the time	Often	Moderately	Occasionally	Rarely

Total your score.

16 or below
  Indicates an organizational climate that is probably high in stress, low in trust, low in morale, ineffective in group discussion, and high in turnover.

17-24 Describes a group on the edge. There is a lot of effective communication occurring but it probably gets inhibited at times by miscommunication or lack of focus in planning.

32 or higher
  Describes a healthy organizational climate. Occasionally miscommunication may be caused by peak demands or high stress, but for the most part, the

CHAPTER FOUR

Developing Communication Competencies

"A key element in determining a manager's potential for advancement is skill in communication...the ability to present ideas and information concisely and effectively, orally, and in writing."

Rawleigh Warner, Jr., Chairman,
Mobil Corporation

When a communication problem occurs, we tend to believe that it was mostly the other people who were responsible, certainly not us. In a survey of 6000 people, William Haney (1973) found that most people felt they communicated "at least as well as and, in many cases, better than everyone else in the organization" (p. 181). When communication broke down, they said that it was "those other people" who were responsible. The "it's not me, it's them" syndrome pervades nearly every area of human involvement. We value listening if the other person is the one who listens. We expect clear speech from others, but don't hold our own messages up to the same standards. But quality communication cannot be solely someone else's responsibility. Creating understanding and promoting dialogue need to be a shared responsibility if we want to achieve a collaborative organizational climate. In the field of interpersonal communication, the following skills are among the most important for building this type of environment. This set of skills is broadly referred to as communication competence.

What is communication competence?

Among the ways scholars have defined communication competence are "the ability to interact well with others" (Spitzberg, 1988, p. 68) and "the ability to manage interaction through performing speech acts and enacting conversations that will produce understanding and/or influence" (Goss & O'Hair, 1988, p. 49). These definitions emphasize that conversational give-and-take produce understanding. We influence each other and trigger reactions through our choice of words. When there is a comfortable balance of speaking and listening, we create understandings that build relationships.

Beth, an employee at a small corporation, wanted to have more open communication with Judy, her new supervisor. A lot of things had been bothering Beth recently, and she wanted management to know how she felt. She finally summoned her courage and knocked on Judy's door. After pleasant greetings, Beth began the conversation. "I don't like the way the personnel policies have been administered lately. I'm feeling a lot of anxiety about these sudden changes."

Judy was new in this job. She wanted to be liked, but also she was concerned about protecting the authority of her position. She reacted to Beth's comment by perceiving that her authority was being challenged. So she responded, "Do you think I'm out to hurt employees? You know these decisions were made with everyone's interest in mind."

For Beth, this triggered a perception that management was closed to employee feelings. In an irritated tone, Beth responded, "I just want to understand why the new policy was carried out like it was. Those of us directly affected by this decision weren't asked about it." Judy thought to herself (self-talk), "They don't like the way I'm doing my job and they don't respect my status." To protect and to emphasize her authority, she replied, "We don't have to explain why. Employees don't need to know everything behind our decisions." Beth felt angry and defensive. She reacted by thinking (self-talk), "They just don't understand. They're closed to our feedback. They want to hurt us." She stood up to leave and simply ended the conversation with, "I guess we'll just have to talk about it later." Both workers had a high commitment to this relationship, but their messages triggered negative self-talk and unconstructive verbal responses.

Scholars have identified as many as 25 separate speaking and listening skill areas that comprise communication competency (Spitzberg & Hurt, 1987). However, for adults in home and work situations, the five dimensions identified by Wiemann nearly 20 years ago still remain the most useful: supportiveness, social relaxation, empathy, flexibility, and interaction management. In the following discussion we will be adding two additional factors to this list: openness and feedback.

Competency 1: Supportiveness

In situations where trust, cooperation, and understanding are important, supportiveness must be regarded as one of the most significant communication competencies. In over twenty years of providing organizational consulting in hospitals, schools, government agencies, and industries, we have found that a lack of supportiveness among staff correlates with almost every form of communication breakdown. Sieberg (1985) describes supportive communication as *confirmation of the other*. This confirmation includes recognizing, acknowledging, endorsing and validating the other person. The kinds of communication behaviors that promote a perception of supportiveness include:

- Statements that acknowledge acceptance of the presence of the other
- Verbal responses that demonstrate understanding and empathy
- Openness to dialogue about the issues as opposed to monologue
- Listening responses that paraphrase, clarify, and summarize
- Verbal expressions delivered with warmth, rather than distance or coldness
- Affirming behaviors such as eye contact and head nods
- Commitment to listen longer before forming judgments
- Providing support publicly and saving criticisms for private conversations.

By comparison, non-supportive statements produce defensiveness and distance from others. Examples include statements of blame, manipulation, and premature judgments, as well as messages that imply superiority, dogmatic certainty and authoritarian control (Gibb, 1961).

Workers usually recognize the necessity of supportiveness. In 1995 Michael Spangle conducted team-building sessions for 45 employees of a regional government organization. The participants identified and then ranked the work issues most important to them. Open communication and supportive communication were selected as two of the top three factors. These workers valued communication that was seen as less critical, less blaming, less controlling, and more valuing. Some pointed out that the lower the job status, the more important supportive communication becomes for job satisfaction.

Listening is more than hearing

One of the ways we demonstrate supportive communication and a desire to relate is through our listening behaviors. Rhodes (1987) found that effective interpersonal communication, including communication by managers, is directly correlated with how well people are perceived as listeners.

Rand Araskog, former Chairman and CEO of ITT, points out the importance of listening:

*As a manager, you make or break your support people by
your attitude. Sometimes it's as simple as taking the time to
listen. You must analyze what's being said; separate the
relevant from the irrelevant; test your understanding of what
you hear; consider the implications; and anticipate — but
don't prejudge — where a particular line of thought is leading.
A manager who learns to listen, enriches the jobs of subordinates by giving them a sense of participation which helps both
them and himself. (Walton, 1989, p. 32)*

Wolvin and Coakley (1985) found that better listening in organizational
communication resulted in fewer mistakes and errors, stronger culture,
greater organizational cohesiveness, more shared viewpoints and perspectives, more successful meetings, and better personnel relationships (p. 15).
Yet in a 1986 survey vice presidential executives from Fortune 500 companies ranked ineffective listening as the second most serious problem in
their organizations (Bennett & Olney, 1986).

Listening involves conscious intent to focus on the message and meaning of another. Stewart and Thomas (1990) propose that effective communication should include *dialogic listening,* "a listening that values and builds
mutuality, requires active involvement, is genuine, and grows out of a
commitment to synergy" (193). Listening that promotes healthy dialogue
is a "two-way process in which two persons reveal, discuss, and extend
the concerns that each party prizes...each feels equally heard by the other"
(Augsburger, 1982, p. 67).

Over the past twenty years, University of Denver professor Alton
Barbour has administered a 20-statement listening survey, entitled "Listening Habits That Irritate Me," to groups from coast-to-coast. Group members surveyed were drawn from industry, hospitals, college classes, the
military, and even the counseling profession. Barbour concluded that
people who perceive that they are not listened to feel discounted and unsupported. Organizations with nonsupportive listeners tend to experience
low morale and less satisfied workers. Barbour finds that groups, regardless of the area of the country or occupations, tend to select the same listening problems on the survey. The top six problems (not in order of priority) are:

1. The other person interrupts me when I talk.
2. The other person never looks at me when I talk. I don't know
   whether he or she is listening or not.

3. The other person treats me as inferior.
4. The other person sits there doing distracting behaviors such as picking at fingernails, cleaning glasses, fidgeting with pencils or paper, instead of listening to me.
5. The other person waits for me to get through talking only so he or she can interject something of his or her own.
6. The other person acts as if he or she is doing me a favor in seeing me and frequently looks at the clock while I'm talking.

This list indicates that distracting behaviors during listening make people feel discounted, as if their contributions don't mean enough to receive full attention. A supportive listener will minimize these intrusive behaviors so that others feel that they are respected and that what they have to say is important.

Characteristics of Supportive Listeners

- Eliminate distractions that might inhibit sufficient attention to the speaker
- Manage self talk in order to give full attention to the messages being heard
- Listen to what isn't being said as an additional component of the message
- Communicate appreciation and respect for the point of view of the speaker even if there is not complete agreement concerning details or meaning
- Listen with eyes, smiles, and body position as well as mind
- Help the other to focus by using questions that narrow broad statements and clarify perceptions
- Minimize premature judgments concerning where the speaker is headed
- Slow down responses to match the speaker's pace and processing of information

---

Mindreading

Supportive listening is frequently inhibited by *mindreading*. This occurs when one person jumps to conclusions about what the other person means, thinks, or is about to say before it's actually spoken. Mindreaders are often guilty of completing the sentences of others or even interrupting others long before explanations are complete. Family therapist David Augsburger (1982) warns, "Mindreading is trespassing. The invasion of another's boundaries violates integrity, usurps responsibility, intrudes on and surrenders the freedom to act as an agent of personal choices" (p. 80).

Suppose your supervisor says, "This report is really late. I needed it yesterday and you're just giving it to me now." With mindreading, your self-talk is, "Boy, am I in trouble. She's saying I failed, but she doesn't understand that it wasn't my fault. The copier broke, the fire alarm kept us out of the building, and I was in meetings for the last two days." There is a possibility that the supervisor isn't being critical at all and in fact appreciated your efforts but your mindreading jumped to a negative conclusion.

Mindreading is a common problem in family relationships as well as in work relationships. For example, a husband says to his wife, "I know we're supposed to go to your mother's on Friday afternoon, but..." She interrupts with, "You don't like my mother, do you? You agreed to take this trip and now you don't want to go." Her mindreading missed the rest of his sentence, "I wonder if we can leave an hour later because of my project deadline." Because she didn't hear him out, he must now defend his commitment to his mother-in-law, as well as explain the actual intent of his message. Mindreading tends to escalate conflict and create feelings of being misunderstood. A supportive listener suppresses the desire to mindread the other and allows more opportunity for explanations.

Problem or predicament?

Counseling psychologist Paul Welter (1978) suggests that listeners will be more effective in providing support if they are aware of the difference between a *problem* and a *predicament*. The term problem, whether personal, organizational, or logistical, implies that information or corrective action can provide an acceptable solution. A predicament refers to a complex and difficult situation for which no single, simple solution will provide a satisfactory answer.

Suppose a colleague says to you, "The copier is broken. What do we do about it?" You respond, "Call Joe in communications. Here's his phone number." You dealt with a problem by giving information that provides a solution. Your child may say, "I haven't finished my report for tomorrow. I couldn't find any information at the school library. What do I do?" You suggest, "I can take you to the city library where I'll help you find the information you need." The child accepts and appreciates this solution to a problem.

Compare the above problems with a friend who says, "There don't seem to be any jobs in this city for my career. Do you think I should look for a job in another state?" You suggest, "Sure, if there's a chance for greater pay or career advancement." Your friend continues, "But I'm worried that my wife won't be able to get work in the type of areas where I need to job hunt." You offer the solution, "Can she possibly work in a different field?" Now your friend become visibly frustrated. "Well, it's just not my wife. What about the kids? They're only half way through high school and they don't want to move. You see my problem?" You try to be helpful saying, "Maybe it's not time for you to move." But your friend acts irritated at your response and says, "But I'm stuck and unhappy in my job. What should I do?" In this scenario, your friend is describing a predicament, a set of problems that cannot be resolved with a single answer.

People in predicaments tend to feel alone and trapped and require unique types of supportive messages, while people with problems are usually looking for specific forms of information. Another distinction is that a predicament is not going to change quickly or in the immediate future. A bad marriage, an undesirable job, aging or ill parents, and having a two-year-old are all examples of situations that may be changed eventually, but won't be eliminated quickly by a simple decision. Welter (1978) summarizes the differences between problems and predicaments:

Problem	Predicament
Information or corrective action can provide a solution	Complex, difficult situation with no single or simple solution
Advice meets no resistance	Advice meets resistance
Single answer provides solution	No solution is apparent
Low involvement with other	A feeling of being alone or trapped
Sense of urgency for solution	Uncomfortable, but no sense of urgency

When someone brings up a problem, he or she is grateful for specific guidance, answers and advice from a listener. When discussing predicaments, people will often respond to apparent gems of wisdom and advice with "yes, but" or "I tried that" statements. Providing answers and advice for problems creates satisfaction in the speaker. However, offering suggestions for predicaments often facilitates a perception of helplessness and anxiety in both speaker and listener. Remember, a predicament is actually a complex set of problems that have no simple solution. About 80%

of the seemingly simple problems people discuss are actually camaflouged complex predicaments. Supportive communication for predicaments requires the ability to help the other dissect, clarify, and process the predicament into solvable problems. Failing to distinguish between the two can be an endless source of frustration for a listener. To respond effectively to a predicament, we must demonstrate *withness* or emotional presence with the other, while problems merely require us to provide knowledge, answers, or advice.

Competency 2: Social Relaxation

For professionals in corporate settings, a second dimension of competency is the ability to create social relaxation. This involves communication behaviors that enable the other to relax in our presence and feel comfortable in communicating with us. People with a strong social relaxation competency fashion a climate of genuineness, acceptance, and emotional safety. They use behaviors that enable others to feel relaxed and comfortable, such as good eye contact, forward leaning posture, and messages that affirm a commitment to relate. A weak competency might be recognized by a distant demeanor, a rigid posture, or harsh tone of voice. Even when it's not intended, speaking with an edge in our voice or sounding tense or unsure might be interpreted by the other as critical or rejecting.

At a city council meeting, a member asked for an increase in the budget. He prefaced his statement with, "This is important for you to understand." Some interpreted his tone to be condescending. Other members bristled, but the speaker appeared unaware that the tone of his message had communicated meaning that he did not intend. When he met unexpected resistance to his request, he didn't appear to understand why. As evidence that *how* we say something may be as important as *what* we say, psychologist Albert Mehrabian points out that attitude is communicated 7% by spoken words, 36% by vocal characteristics, and 55% by nonverbal behaviors (Mehrabian & Weiner, 1967).

Koermer, Goldstein and Fortson (1993) conducted a study using instructions such as, "Describe a conversation you had with your immediate supervisor in which he or she helped you feel comfortable." They found satisfying perceptions were associated with expressions of personal interest in subordinates, expressions of confidence in a subordinate's ability, verbal and nonverbal attentiveness, willingness to assist a subordinate, and verbal appreciation for commendable work. Conversely, workers associated dissatisfaction with factors such as disregard for subordinate input, supervisor statements that demeaned subordinates, lack of verbal or nonverbal attentiveness, and overly restricting control of a subordinate's communication. Additionally, participants identified nonverbal behaviors which reduced comfort levels such as shuffling papers rather than paying attention, having blank looks, or answering the phone while talking to them.

Decentering

An important aspect of social relaxation is the ability to focus our attention on the other, or to *decenter*. Examples of decentering include looking at the other person when talking, showing approval through head nods and "uh huhs," referring to the other person often, and complimenting the other. Wiemann (1977) states that "the competent communicator is one who is other oriented, while at the same time maintaining the ability to accomplish his or her own goals" (p. 198).

At times, creating an atmosphere of social relaxation so that the other will communicate involves finding the right topic to discuss or common ground to emphasize. A hospital chaplain told how he used to work with difficult patients who wouldn't respond to hospital staff. One particular patient, a 70-year-old named Jake, would not cooperate with life saving treatments or communicate with hospital personnel. He appeared ready to die. The chaplain spent the first part of his visit watching staff interact with Jake. A nursing staff member approached Jake and requested him to do something. When he ignored her, she tried to order him and force his cooperation. Neither tactic moved Jake to action. When she was gone, the chaplain sat down in front of Jake. After a few questions that brought no response, the chaplain noticed on the chart that Jake was from Montana. He tried another approach. "I see that you are from Montana. I once worked up there near an Indian reservation. Ever heard of it?" Jake lifted up his head and spent the next 20 minutes telling the chaplain about his years on the railroad, his work on that same reservation, and his love for the prairie. When the nursing staff came back, they found Jake openly conversant and ready to begin treatments. The chaplain had used his ability to decenter (his needs, not mine), and created a climate of sharing that eventually facilitated a relationship and treatment for this patient.

Physical congruence

Physical congruence is another technique that establishes an accepting climate for relating and openness for listening. When we squarely face an individual during a conversation, we communicate that we are attentively listening. As our body turns away at 45 or 90 degree angles, we create the perception that we are not paying attention to speakers. Listeners who sit physically congruent to speakers receive a greater quantity and higher quality of verbal statements than those who sit at angles.

Warm-up

Another skill that enhances social relaxation involves *warm-up*, or the ability to ease into a discussion. Warm-up creates a transition which helps us to disengage from where we've been and prepare for where we are. A supervisor recently shared an experience with me.

> After being in budget meetings all morning, I returned to my office. I had my lunch in one hand and my briefcase in the other. Before I could set anything down, a colleague walked in and asked for some complex information and an immediate decision on a question. I snapped at her, 'not now,' and turned to set down the papers in my hands. Later, I realized my sharpness and apologized to her. But I wished that she had been sensitive to where I was mentally when she came into my office.

Insufficient warm-up (as well as overly prolonged warm-up) facilitates higher anxiety and greater potential for miscommunication. High activity work environments often don't allow for sufficient transition and warm-up, creating highly stressed communicators and less satisfying exchanges of information. The ability to provide sufficient warm-up is an important skill for reducing unnecessary anxiety between communicators.

Warm-up may be as simple as a few minutes of small talk about the weekend, the kids, or the latest events in sports. It enables us to be emotionally and mentally present instead of thinking about the last board meeting or the traffic on the way to work. Most of us need a few minutes to readjust before hearing difficult questions or being asked to make decisions. Taking time for warm-up will create more attentiveness in relationships and a greater willingness to listen.

Competency 3: Empathy

In corporations, we frequently hear comments such as, "They ask questions, but don't listen to our answers," or "We just don't count around here." As Cronkite (1976) emphasizes, "Empathy is both a cause and an effect of successful communication; in fact, cause and effect in this case blend so completely that in a broad sense we can say that empathy is communication" (p. 80). Gordon (1988) found that empathetic understanding contributes to greater job satisfaction and lower employee turnover. More importantly, for those who work on staffs, empathy promotes prosocial behavior and greater communication responsiveness (Stiff, et al., 1988).

Communication with empathy involves suppressing our inner self-talk and agenda long enough to acknowledge another's presence. Empathy sends the message that we hear what the other is saying and validate the importance of what the other person feels. This doesn't assume agreement with the other's feelings, only that the feelings have been heard and respected. Psychologist Carl Rogers (1990) says that empathy occurs when listeners take time to "hear the words, the thoughts, the feeling tones" and "sense the shape of the other person's inner world" (p. 439). Empathy promotes open communication, more positive interaction, and less tension.

Exercise physiologist Vicki Siegel-Makowka, who works with cardiac rehabilitation patients at a Denver hospital, points out that, "empathy allows the patient to feel less isolated. It establishes rapport and opens doors so that people don't feel so vulnerable. It helps us understand their priorities and where they're coming from. Empathy helps people overcome fear and facilitates a willingness to modify behavior."

Empathy can easily be inhibited by dogmatic thinking or a rigidly judgmental orientation. Hearing the other becomes difficult if we are not open to new information or if we believe that the other doesn't meet our expectations or personal standard.

Characteristics of Empathetic Communication

- Messages reflect a commitment to understanding the other's point of view
- Feelings are validated even though we may not agree with the feelings
- Presence and contributions of the other are accepted
- Attention is given to the meaning behind the words expressed by the other

---

Being in sync

For a machine to run smoothly, the gears and mechanisms need to be in sync, or harmonious and balanced. Being *in sync* in a conversation occurs when we are able to demonstrate physical congruence as well as emotional presence. Cognitively or emotionally, we stand with the other as he or she explores an issue. Being in sync with the other promotes freedom of expression and depth when we are looking at the issues. Being *out of sync* causes an atmosphere in which the other is not sure whether we can be trusted and may fear that we will unfairly judge his or her approach to an issue. Being out of sync shows in comments such as:

- *Where's your head today?*
- *You're not getting the picture yet.*
- *It's difficult to talk to you. Your mind is somewhere else today.*

Fatigue and preoccupation cause many of the struggles with being out of sync. Sometimes we catch ourselves and respond with comments such as, "I'm sorry, I'm just not with it today. I've had a lot on my mind." If we're aware that we're out of sync with a speaker, it's better to admit it and indicate what we're thinking about. This prevents the listener from thinking that we don't like him or her or that we're apathetic toward the issue.

Commitment to respecting and understanding the feelings of another in a professional setting is a challenge. Projects and tasks may drain our available energy, and we rarely get rewarded for taking time to understand the perspective of another. But empathy, as a component of validating and caring communication, "helps organization members cope with the many stresses and ambiguities of organizational life, achieve, reorient themselves, adapt, and grow" (Kreps, 1990, p. 163).

Compentency 4: Behavioral Flexibility

Corporate needs and expectations change quickly, often requiring on-the-spot ability to adapt communication to the situation. Behavioral flexibility refers to this ability to change our style or alter our words to respond to an immediate need. Psychologist Milton Rokeach (1960) describes the orientation that undergirds flexibility as

> *the extent to which the person [listener] can receive, evaluate, and act on relevant information received from outside on the basis of its own intrinsic merits, unencumbered by irrelevant factors in the situation arising from within the person or from the outside. (p. 57)*

At US West Cellular, this competency is considered important enough that job interviewers assess the ability of applicants to adjust their approach to match the needs of the task. This includes shifting priorities to meet changing demands and "think on your feet" skills by adapting communication to the situation.

Behavioral flexibility involves reducing language that demonstrates an "all or nothing" perspective. Terms such as *always, never, all,* or *none,* give way to words like *sometimes, possibly, usually,* and *normally* (Weaver, 1987, p. 161). All-or-nothing language will often minimize complex issues, forcing us into dogmatic thinking. In some corporate settings, managers leave no room for discussion, giving us the message, "It's either my way or the highway."

Flexibility becomes inhibited by psychological factors such as the need to bolster ego, ingrained habits, and an overbearing need for control or power. Inflexible communicators apply programmed expectations and demands to their relationships, as if there's only one way to do or see things, "their way." Northwestern University professors of organizational communication Max Bazerman and Margaret Neale (1992) characterize this as *psychological anchoring*, an unswerving commitment to a way of thinking and behaving. Psychological anchoring inhibits the ability to adapt communication to the needs of the moment. Because of unrealistic expectations or commitments or precedents, the inflexible communicator frustrates creative problem solving or full consideration of new possibilities.

Balancing control in relationships

To increase competence in behavioral flexibility, we must begin with balancing control in relationships. The inflexible communicator tries to control others in several ways:

- Thoughts: "You shouldn't think that way"
- Communication: "Don't talk that way"
- Decreasing alternatives: "I can't bear thinking about doing it any other way."

Relinquishing or balancing control requires listening longer, valuing the relationship enough to give input a fair hearing, and promoting feelings of partnership and inclusion. We have to consciously avoid using the same unbending attitudes or behavioral patterns we've always worked with and to entertain a greater range of choices and options.

One manager told me he put a sign that says "Listen Longer" on the wall right behind the spot where employees stand when they come to him with questions or concerns. This reminds him to hold his judgment and responses long enough to be sure he's heard the whole story.

Trigger words

Sanders (1995) points out that communication competence includes the ability, "to monitor the progress of an interaction and fashion responses with effective remedial steps if it heads in the wrong direction" (p. 118). Our communication behaviors both trigger and are triggered by the behaviors of others. A supervisor was upset when an employee asked, "Why does management feel a need to exploit employees?" The only word the supervisor heard was "exploit." Because of her negative associations with people who exploit others, the impact of the message was, "I'm the enemy." Another manager says that the phrases, "You don't listen," or "You don't care," push her hot-button and she hears very little that follows. Another manager became furious when he received an e-mail stating, "You're not doing things right lately," words that for him were synonymous with failure. Manning and Curtis (1988) explain that red flag words create "emotional deaf spots," causing people to quit listening (p. 27). By monitoring our choice of words and the effect on our listeners, we can recognize negative associations and reframe our statements. Consider the impact of saying, "I'm not sure I was clear with what I said. Let me state it in a different way."

In many work settings, there are individuals who use trigger words as a technique for manipulation. At the right moment, they use a word or phrase as a tool to create fear or anxiety. An employee shared, "A manager came to me the other day and said that I was incompetent because I didn't meet his deadline. I was devastated that someone would call me incompetent." These communication triggers push us into automatic, defensive responses. We lose our ability to be flexible and respond effectively. Recognizing these words and our negative associations helps us disarm them. We might ask ourselves, "What question could I ask that would determine what he or she really means?"

Nadia Younes, Human Resources Manager and Director of Diversity Initiatives for Norwest Banks, recommends that we mentally "put people's language thorough a sieve and get at the intent of their message rather than just acknowledging the impact. We need to take responsibility for our own reaction and not be triggered by the message." We can disarm troubling statements by listening for the message behind the words that are used.

Perfectionism

Perfectionism is another enemy of behavioral flexibility. In education and job tasks, we are rewarded for being thorough and giving great attention to details. In interpersonal communication this often has a much different outcome. Perfectionistic people sometimes withhold feelings and opinions because they can't say them perfectly. Relationships suffer intense pressure when one member continually feels judged or unable to meet expectations. In interpersonal relationships at the workplace or at home, we have to allow for imperfections and mistakes. It's okay to say something several times before we get the point right. It's okay to misspeak, especially if we speak again with more clarity. It's okay to have holes in our understanding and to need more explanations or a review of procedures. In our work with cardiac rehabilitation patients, we discovered that perfectionism was a consistent trait. Most of these middle-aged professionals applied a standard of perfection to both their jobs and their relationships. Now they were worn out by the frustrations and failures caused by unrealistic standards. We teach them to live under a new concept in their lives, "It doesn't have to be perfect in order to be good."

Competency 5: Interaction Management

Many of us have participated in meetings where someone talks longer than we have the tolerance to listen. Sometimes we get involved in conversations where the topic becomes boring and we have a difficult time changing the subject. Interaction competence addresses issues of quantity, quality, relevance, and balance in discussions. In an effectively managed conversation, each person perceives that he or she is making sufficient contributions. We need to ask ourselves, "Do I create an atmosphere that encourages people to talk to me or give me honest feedback?" We must cultivate awareness of the impact of our choice of words or our attitudes. Harris (1993) points out that "the litmus test for effective interaction management is if people feel comfortable being around you most of the time" (p. 300).

Conversation that facilitates relationships

Grice (1989), formerly a professor of philosophy at the University of California Berkeley, has identified four maxims of conversation that facilitate a cooperative relationship for achieving a common purpose or goal:

1. *Quantity: Sharing the appropriate amount of information*
   Our goal is to provide responses that are neither too brief nor too wordy. Lashbrook and Lashbrook (1975) found that listeners focus best if messages do not exceed 45 seconds. In addition, speakers will be most effective if they pay attention to listener cues indicating that they've gone too long. When quantity exceeds listening patience, a receiver's eyes begin to look distant; he or she fidgets impatiently, begins to turn away, and stops focusing on the message. If a speaker turns a response into a speech, it might be helpful to interrupt and ask if you can clarify or summarize points.

2. *Quality: Messages perceived as truthful*
   When messages reflect honest intentions or offer claims supported by evidence, they are regarded as truthful. Manipulative or truth-bending statements may lead to a high degree of distrust or suspicion. The quality of our communication shapes our reputation and may influence future interaction. Once we lose a reputation for honesty, we find this reputation difficult to regain. For example, in a series of training sessions in team communications at one company, participants engaged in role playing to practice negotiating. In these simulations, many gained negative reputations because of the way they treated colleagues to achieve the goals. Interestingly, these reputations carried over into their real work settings and remained resistant to change for many months.

3. *Relevance: Communication appropriate to the needs of the moment*
Messages should be relevant to the needs of the moment. Communication that is irrelevant or tangential to the subject at hand may be interpreted as unconcerned or unknowledgeable. Consider the following conversation which actually occurred in a Denver hospital:

Nurse: I was uncomfortable with how you spoke to me in front of the last patient.

Doctor: I sure haven't appreciated nurses on the other floor talking about me in such a negative manner. They ought to be replaced.

The nurse later shared her frustration with another worker, saying, "He just doesn't get it." The unrelated responses by the doctor were interpreted by the nurses as rejecting and uncaring. From the physician's point of view, he was disclosing anxiety and emotional pain, but his timing was poor. By his inattentiveness to the nurse's topic of concern, he reinforced perceptions that he didn't care what she thought.

4. *Manner: Messages that are clear and well organized*
Effective communicators provide messages that are clear, well-organized, and unambiguous. In today's public relations effort, airline companies may refer to accidents as "involuntary conversions," businesses characterize lay-offs as "management-initiated attrition," prison officials refer to prisoners as "clients of the correctional systems," and the Postal Service describes fired employees as "excessed out." Ambiguous terms may serve a purpose but they also frustrate and anger listeners. When work responsibilities and expectations are ambiguous, job performance and employee satisfaction tend to be lower.

Competency 6: Openness

Brown and Van Riper (1981) propose that the essential principle of speech in a relationship is "that one reveals, not conceals...we should disclose, not enclose" (p. 342). The factor of openness lies somewhere between a trait and a competency, and strongly impacts interpersonal relationships and quality of work. Communication professor Carl Larson (1995) at the University of Denver performed a meta-analysis of 100 studies of team communication, both empirical and relational dimensions. The factors of openness and affiliative behavior (warmth toward the other) combined to explain 67% of the quality of the outcomes.

The ability to share information in an honest and genuine manner may be a trait, but knowing when and where to share that information is a competency. Brown and Van Riper (1981) add that we are not suggesting "a philosophy of openness that means indiscriminately saying everything to everybody...we should not say that which is destructive to community relationships" (p. 343). Openness in sharing information requires that the speaker meet several criteria: appropriate timing, appropriate context, sensitivity of the speaker to the feelings and opinions of the other, and reasonable and safe risks for disclosure.

Openness involves sending a message that we understand the perspective of the other, communicating that we are receptive to new, relevant information, and implying that we are willing to consider mutually acceptable alternatives. A dogmatic or rigid stance may win the short-term battle of getting our way, but lose relationships in the long-term. We all need to win an occasional disagreement and maintain a perception of control. However, supervisors or colleagues who are determined that their perspective is always best and that their way is the right way, shut out the potential of new and possibly better approaches. Open-minded people allow room for new possibilities and communicate their commitment to at least hear the other's perspective.

Qualities of Open-Minded Workers

- Send messages that emphasize "ours" instead of "mine"
- Minimize statements that reflect positional orientations and employ more statements that seek underlying interests, needs, and the perspective of the other
- Suspend premature judgments in order to hear the full perspective of the other
- Demonstrate respect for the opinion and perspective of the other
- Communicate with genuineness and sincerity
- Understand that issues have gray areas that need to be explored

---

In our work with corporations, employees frequently complain, "Management doesn't want to hear our input. They already have their minds made up, so why should I bother saying anything?" Openness facilitates a climate of mutual sharing, trust, honesty, genuineness, and cooperation. Alternately, a closed attitude breeds suspicion, hidden agendas, deception, distrust, and competitiveness. Not surprisingly, a survey of patients at Texas medical clinics found that patients expressed more satisfaction with doctors who demonstrated candor, warmth, and empathy, but expressed a lack of satisfaction with physicians who were controlling and domineering (Adler et al., 1989, p. 263).

Competency 7: Feedback

Giving and receiving feedback, although sometimes difficult, must be regarded as an essential competency in corporate, as well as family communication. Effective managers use feedback as a tool for maintaining trusting relationships, assuring that messages are clearly understood, and clarifying organizational objectives. Cusella (1987) regards feedback as, "central to an understanding of organizational behavior in general and of organizational communication specifically" (p. 624).

Feedback is the set of messages, positive or negative, that senders receive in response to the messages they have sent. It is the vehicle for monitoring the effectiveness of our communication choices and guiding us in making periodic adjustments. "The underlying power of feedback lies in its capacity to validate the assumptions, constructs, and ideas we have about other people's actions" (Harris, 1993, p. 252).

Feedback includes two components: giving and receiving. Floyd (1985) points out that giving genuine, accurate, and positive feedback facilitates "the establishment of a supportive psychological climate" (p. 125). Feedback that contributes to a supportive climate promotes greater worker satisfaction and more effective organizations.

Guidelines for Giving Effective Feedback

- Discuss behavior or tasks; don't attack or evaluate the competency or the personality of the person
- Give affirmation honestly, in a genuine manner, without ulterior motives
- Provide feedback as soon as possible when it's related to a specific action
- Be specific with clear explanations and realistic suggestions
- Invite questions and allow responses from the receivers about how the feedback affects them
- Give corrective feedback privately
- Avoid giving feedback "in the heat of battle." At such times we tend to overstate what we mean or the other person misperceives our meaning

---

Inability to receive feedback can harm relationships in families as well as corporations, sometimes with devastating results. John, a psychologist, received an urgent call one evening from a police officer friend. A family disagreement with the officer's 15-year-old daughter had escalated into threats of violence. When John arrived at the friend's home, he tried to reason with the family, but the father was furious. He announced, "Teenagers don't respect or listen to adults. They're not willing to learn other ways of seeing things. They are closed to input." John asked the daughter for her perspective. She started to explain her view of the situation, but her father immediately interrupted with, "See how closed-minded they are! Teenagers just don't listen." John tried to intercede saying, "But you didn't let her finish what she was saying." Twice more the daughter began to speak and both times the father interrupted with more complaints about teenagers. Later that night, the daughter ran away from home. She left on her pillow a note that read, "I'm leaving to find someone who will listen."

Effective feedback requires openness in both the one who sends the message, and the one who receives it. In the above example, the father wanted to give feedback about the behavior of his daughter, but he didn't want to hear any feedback about his own behavior. If others perceive that we are open to suggestions, they exhibit a greater receptivity to our ideas and opinions as well. In a sense we model the kind of attitude that we'd like to see in others.

Giving negative feedback

Corrective or negative feedback requires sensitivity to issues of timing and the emotional state of the receiver. Early Monday morning when people are re-adjusting to work, receptivity to suggestions may be low. Late in the afternoon, when colleagues are tired, there may be an unwillingness to listen to different ways of doing things. To decrease the potential for defensive or counterproductive reactions, we may need to save feedback until there's adequate time for response and discussion.

When feedback is poorly received, consider the possibility that life events, illness, or family relationships might be affecting the person's ability to listen to suggestions. Receptivity may be improved by first spending a few minutes asking how things are going in the person's life. Others will be more willing to hear our feedback if they believe we understand and care about them.

Fear of penalty for honest feedback is unfortunately common in many organizational settings. At a large community college, employees often made comments like, "I wouldn't dare go to personnel or administration with this, because I'd be docked in my performance appraisal." One employee was simply told, "If you don't like what we do here, go elsewhere."

If others feel there will be reprisals for giving us feedback, they will be less than honest. Whether our setting is family or work, there will be more distrust, lower morale, and lower quality relationships if we are not able to provide a climate of safety for others to share feedback. We may not be able to utilize all suggestions, but we can affirm the speaker and at least demonstrate a small measure of response. As telecommunications manager Bill Chapman points out, being able to receive negative feedback is very important. "My long-term success depends on my employees, not on me. I recognize that my opinions are probably right between 60-65% of the time. That means that sometimes I'm not on target. I'm foolish not to listen to other people's views including negative or critical feedback on my ideas."

Coping with negative feedback

We can improve our ability to handle difficult feedback by mentally separating the words from the person who says them. Practicing this skill may help maintain smoother relationships because we change defensive reactions into an ability to listen without making immediate judgments.

As a first step in listening to negative feedback, organizational consultant Don Walton (1989) recommends, "On complex or especially important matters, be sure that what you think the other party said is what he or she really meant" (p. 82). Effective responses to feedback involve making statements that demonstrate a commitment to clarification and understanding.

Questions work well because they can be non-threatening and de-escalate negative emotions. For example, you might say, "What can we do to make this right?" or "Help me understand what we should do differently." To manage negative self-talk, ask yourself, "How much of what this person is saying is his or her stress and how much actually involves my behavior?" Patience and understanding will often defuse negative aspects of the situation and move us beyond reactive and critical responses. If we can listen longer and manage our stress when we receive negative feedback, others will be grateful for our willingness to understand their concerns.

Ways to Cope with Negative Feedback

- Disarm negative, trigger words by reframing them in your self-talk. Allow the possibilities that the words have many different meanings and that maybe you haven't clearly understood what the message sender meant.
- Reduce the perception of threat. Is my safety *really* threatened or am I overreacting?
- Don't jump to conclusions. You may be drawing implications which are not accurate. Don't let assumptions prejudge the message until you have more information.
- Use silence as a technique. Silence allows the other person time to rephrase or clarify meaning. Waiting longer before you respond also allows you to defuse emotional triggers and be in greater control of your response.
- Keep focused on the goal of understanding the other person, not judging. Your choice of goal, understanding or judgment, may determine whether there is a positive or negative outcome to the conversation.
- Disconnect your ego or self-esteem from the message. For some people, giving feedback is as difficult as hearing it. Realize that their statements are a reflection of their perception and not a commentary on your worth. What you hear may be their pain rather than an accurate assessment of your ability.

Personal Assessment of Communication Skills

Rate yourself on each of the following statements. Score yourself a 5 if this statement describes you most of the time, 4 if it's often, 3 if it occurs some of the time, 2 if it rarely occurs, and 1 if it never occurs.

_____ 1. In conversation, I listen about the same amount of time as I talk.

_____ 2. I am able to shut-out distractions caused by other people, activities, or sounds when I am listening to some talk.

_____ 3. People regard me as warm and friendly, as opposed to cold and distant.

_____ 4. I listen fully to what another's saying and try to understand their point of view before I begin to argue.

_____ 5. I ask a lot of questions when someone is talking to show that I'm interested in what they're saying and to help them develop their ideas.

_____ 6. People regard me as someone who is honest and genuine when I am talking with them.

_____ 7. People appear to be comfortable with me when we engage in conversation.

_____ 8. Rarely do I have to explain things a second time because someone misunderstood me.

_____ 9. I smile a lot when I talk.

_____ 10. I explain issues and problems in a clear and organized manner.

_____ 11. I appreciate and affirm others when I'm engaged in conversations.

_____ 12. Rarely do I interrupt others while they're speaking.

_____ 13. I make a lot of eye contact when I talk to someone.

_____ 14. In discussions, I am able to be flexible on issues even if I disagree with someone.

_____ 15. I find that I can talk with just about anyone about a lot of different subjects.

_____ 16. When someone else is talking, I focus more on what they're saying rather than on what I am going to say next.

_____ 17. People frequently confide in me about issues important to them.

_____ 18. I resist mindreading or jumping to conclusions so that I can understand the whole issue before making a judgment.

_____ 19. When I disagree with someone, I am able to negotiate agreements effectively.

_____ 20. In conversations, I effectively control my nonverbal communication, such as looking away a lot, fidgeting, or speaking in a tone of voice that might be regarded as demeaning.

Scores of 80-100 describe a person who builds strong relationships based on listening, supportive behaviors, clarify of messages, and balanced speaking and listening. Scores of 60-79 describe someone who has a few areas to work on, such as listening longer, reserving judgment until all is heard, focusing greater warmth as a personality style and greater acceptance of others' viewpoints. Scores of 40-59 describe someone who needs to decenter more (look at issues from the viewpoints of others), work on more affirming nonverbal messages such as smiles and head nods that encourage, and demonstrate a stronger commitment to mutual understanding.

CHAPTER FIVE

Communication Channels between Supervisors and Employees

Employees often tell us they hate their jobs. When asked why, invariably the reasons include abusive management communication, unrealistic expectations with minimal resources, and very little positive feedback or appreciation. These communication styles may appear to managers to be getting the job done, but they often contribute to burnout and even physical illness as well as destroying morale and breeding intense resentment toward management.

Communication style influences relationships and productivity at all levels within an organization. Supervisors that change an authoritarian, harsh, or demanding style to more supportive and affirming techniques usually see equal if not better work outcomes, with lower stress levels and more positive perceptions of the organization.

Negative communication style: A case study

Mark is a project supervisor at a large appliance manufacturing firm. He recently described the managerial communication during the development and completion of a major project. At the initial planning meeting for the new appliance, Mark was excited. He presented his department's design concept for a revolutionary new oven that would be utilized by commercial food outlets such as fast food restaurants. He pointed out that preliminary studies indicated there would be a high demand for the appliance from the moment it became available in production.

Understandably, management determined it wanted quick development of the project to allow delivery and subsequent sales revenue as soon as possible. Mark's engineering team went to work immediately. They began to devise a timeline, carefully analyzing and planning the sequential steps involved.

Because he understood the company's urgency, Mark streamlined the process wherever he could, cutting corners, planning tight production schedules, and begging suppliers to agree to speed shipment of parts. After including every possible shortcut, Mark determined a somewhat risky but feasible timeline of 12 months.

As he laid the proposal on his manager's desk, Mark experienced a brief moment of pride at suggesting the phenomenal goal. The vice president scanned it quickly, threw it down, and announced, "This won't do. I want this oven available for shipment in six months." Mark was aghast. "But I've worked this proposal to the bone and I can't cut it any further. I don't see any possible way to complete it in six months."

"Well, that's what must be done to keep this company financially viable. What will it take to do this? Do you need more help? What if you had 30 engineers on your team instead of four? If I get you the resources, can you can get it done?" Even though he believed it would be impossible, Mark stammered, "I don't know. I'll meet with my team and discuss the options." The vice president announced, "Well, I'll expect to see your new timeline next week. And remember, if you can't figure out how to get this project done on time, I'll find someone who will."

Mark went back to his team and they brainstormed every possible way to shorten the timeline. They determined that additional staff might enable them to divide some of the tasks into sections so they could accomplish several development stages simultaneously. They also called suppliers and cajoled, begged, and manipulated to assure faster delivery of critical parts. After factoring in every possible change, they shortened the timeline by two months.

With trepidation, Mark presented the revised proposal to the vice president. He knew the new timeline contained variables that he didn't have control over, as well as risk factors that could jeopardize quality of the product. However, the vice president again was still not satisfied. He handed it back, saying "This is a good start. I'll work on assigning additional engineers to the project while you go back and create ways to shave four more months off the deadline. Can you do that?" Mark sank into his chair and groaned, "I'll do my best."

Mark and his team started the project. They began working 14-hour days, often adding weekend time as well. They anxiously waited for the additional staff. However, the company never followed through with its promise, and the team remained at four engineers.

In the meantime, the vice president told his sales staff that Mark was moving the deadline up and thought he could have the product ready in six months. So the sales people began presenting the potential appliance to the restaurants in their territories. To appease the buyers, they assured early production and began taking large orders for the oven units. Soon the word was getting back to the vice president that this appliance was a huge success and he began pressuring Mark even more.

In his efforts to force the engineering team to work harder and faster, the vice president tried a lot of tactics. He scheduled meetings at unusual hours like 6:30 a.m. or 8:00 p.m. to be sure the staff was working long hours. He belittled Mark and his staff in front of division group meetings, saying things like, "If this project had just one good engineer, it would be on time. This company can't survive without that oven produced on time. If we go under, it will be your fault."

When Mark protested that he had never received the promised additional staff, the vice president responded with, "Are you saying your team isn't competent? If you can't make that deadline, just turn in your resignation and I'll find some one who will." He then demanded more frequent detailed reports that further cut into Mark's time.

As the initial deadline approached, it became clear that the oven wasn't ready for production. The vice president escalated his threats, "You are going to cost the company $1.5 million by missing that deadline. I hope you've got your resumé polished. You're going to need it if this doesn't go on schedule." Sometimes he turned to manipulation: "Why don't you instruct your engineers to skip some of the testing steps? You could probably start the assembly line a few weeks before receiving the government agency approvals. You know they'll eventually be in place, so no one will know the difference."

During the next few months of the project, Mark and his staff were subjected to almost daily assaults in the vice president's attempt to make them work harder and faster in order to produce more. The staff tried. Out of dedication to their work and fear for their futures, they battled fatigue, headaches, ulcers and panic attacks to keep pushing on the project. Their home lives suffered, and badly needed social outlets like golf or other exercise disappeared.

The company finally began shipping the ovens eight months after the project began. In its wake was a beleaguered team whose members hated their boss, their company, and occasionally even each other. Furthermore, early shipments of the product were plagued with problems that might have been prevented if more time had been spent on adequate testing and quality assurance.

Mark summarized the issues, "Management made arbitrary decisions, like demanding the completion of the project in half the time, with no perception of what was required to build this product. They never seemed to listen when we explained that the steps had to be done sequence. They wanted us to do testing on a model that wasn't built, order parts that weren't designed yet, and skip requirements that were government dictated. Fear was always their primary tactic. They threatened to fire us, and assured us that if the project failed, the company will be financially ruined and it would all be our fault!"

This hard-driving vice president demonstrated many of the behaviors that challenge and frustrate supervisors and staff members in corporations.

Negative communications patterns

- Lack of understanding of necessary resources for getting jobs done
- Mixed messages about the task or project or priorities
- Constant sense of urgency, regardless of task
- Minimal consideration of emotional or physical impact on staff
- Insistence on reaching goals, but not providing adequate resources

---

Negative communication patterns are often counterproductive, and result in anger and resentment rather than getting more work out of employees. However, whether you supervise others or work as part of an equal team, you *can* influence the communication styles in your company. This chapter will focus on two levels of communication within organizations:

1. *Downward communication*
   Messages to those lower in rank. Goals include supporting, directing, instructing and persuading subordinates.
2. *Upward communication*
   Messages to those with higher rank. Goals include influencing, understanding, and supporting the work goals of superiors.

The power of positive managerial communication

Several dimensions of managerial interpersonal communication impact the quality of relationships and the productivity of workers, but five of the most important dimensions are:

1. Appreciating employee efforts
2. Clarifying organizational information
3. Maintaining communication links
4. Developing channels for upward influence
5. Facilitating shared understandings of tasks and responsibilities

These dimensions will be discussed in detail from the perspective of downward communication, or efforts that can be made by managers at all levels. You may recognize overlap with other levels as well, including influencing those over you or maintaining good relationships with peers.

Appreciating employee efforts

In Mark's manufacturing company, employees were apparently viewed as commodities that could be manipulated for company goals. A study conducted at the University of Michigan Institute for Social Research examined the management differences between groups, based on productivity. They found that supervisors in highly productive groups treated employees "more as people than as things, animals, or machines for turning out products" (Cushman & Cahn, 1985, p. 102). Supervisors in lower producing groups were more critical in their communication, often conveying a message of punishment. The demanding vice president of the manufacturing firm managed to force higher productivity, but his gains will be temporary and may be costly in terms of long-term worker commitment and morale. Fernando Bartolome (1993), professor of management at Bentley College, points out that in the interpersonal communication between managers and their staff, "the law of reciprocity tends to rule. When supervisors use a lot of fine words about trust and respect but behave disdainfully, subordinates are likely to respond in kind" (p. 9).

Creating happy employees

Karen has worked as a receptionist for the same dentist for the last 15 years. During this time both the office staff and the technical staff have stayed consistent, with almost no turnover. Karen says, "I'm glad to come to work every day. I don't mind working late or weekends if that's what it takes to get the job done." When asked what the secret was for such a satisfied, hardworking staff, she identified three principles that characterize her work environment:

1. *Equality*
   My boss treats me with equality, even though other dentists tell him he should be more authoritarian with his staff.
2. *Humor*
   My boss has a great sense of humor. We get along with each other as friends.
3. *Appreciation*
   I don't think there has been a single night where my boss didn't say "Thank you" before I left. He's appreciative. It makes me want to work later than I have to or come in at other times to get the job done.

In contrast, it's difficult to work for managers who don't appreciate our efforts. A staff member once complained to me, "In my annual job evaluation, there was no mention of a single accomplishment this past year. I guess I know what they think of me." With employees frequently being asked to do more with less, comments that express appreciation must be a first step in good managerial communication.

International management consultants Ed Oakley and Doug Krug (1991) report that, in a US Department of Commerce study, appreciation was ranked as the most important factor employees wanted from supervisors. In that same study, in direct contrast, managers ranked appreciation as eighth in importance. Supervisors need to raise this value to a higher priority and send clearer messages that show they care about what employees think and that they appreciate their efforts.

Clarifying organizational information

Because there are many layers of management and tasks that cross departmental boundaries, employees often receive multiple, ambiguous, and sometimes conflicting messages. Kreps (1990) warns, "Many directions are hurriedly communicated and vaguely stated leaving workers unsure about what it is they are being directed to do...contradictory downward communication messages can frustrate workers and thereby damage organizational morale" (p. 204). One employee indicated that in a typical day he receives ten pages of memos, 15 phone-mail messages, 25 e-mail messages, and ten or more phone calls. When he adds the organizational directives and meeting summaries, the employee has to sort through a great deal of information. An important responsibility for managers is to bring clarity and assess priority to the information employees receive.

Lack of clarity in organizational directives and decisions is magnified as it passes down the chain of command. Sometimes senior level managers can help deliver messages to the lower levels of the organization, demonstrating commitment to all workers and reducing message distortion. For example, the chairman of United Airlines one year flew more than 20,000 miles to meet directly with employees. Jack Welch, CEO of General Electric, advises that good managers engage in "eyeball-to-eyeball" communication, which means "Do more listening than talking. Don't just make pronouncements on videotape or announcements in a newspaper. You need to go up, down and around the organization to reach people; make a religion of being accessible" (Tichy & Charan, 1993, p. 222).

If you aren't monitoring the clarification of information, you may unknowingly cause stress and dissatisfaction in what would ordinarily be a strong staff. Chris Argyris (1993), Professor Emeritus at the Harvard School of Business and Education, identifies (tongue in cheek) four steps that are guaranteed to bring *chaos* in executive communication:

1. Design a clearly ambiguous message
2. Ignore any inconsistencies in the message
3. Make the ambiguity and inconsistency in the message undiscussable
4. Make the undiscussability also undiscussable. (p. 20-21)

Unfortunately, many organizations unintentionally follow these steps, contributing to increased tension on staffs, perceptions of incompetence, and employee discouragement. Management on every level will enhance staff performance by rooting out inconsistencies and giving messages clearer focus.

Maintaining communication links

Managers who serve as communication bridges or links between people and networks can help maintain strong channels within an organization. "By virtue of interpersonal contacts, both with subordinates and with a network of contacts, the manager emerges as the nerve center of the organizational unit" (Mintzberg, 1987, p. 423). A manager serves as a monitor who continually scans the environment for beneficial information, and as a disseminator who makes the information available to staff. Organizational troubles often relate to a perception that there are only two groups of workers, "us and them," or higher management and lower staff employees. This gap can be narrowed by more managers serving as bridges between organizational groups.

During 1995, a national banking firm's 93 senior managers participated in research to identify characteristics of 120 of their most successful mid-level managers. The six characteristics most consistently identified were:

1. Connecting people with the organizational vision
2. Articulating clear expectations
3. Fostering open dialogue
4. Respecting employees
5. Providing a balanced, consistent approach in supervision
6. Demonstrating a "can do" positive attitude

Three of the six qualities speak directly to the importance of a supervisor's role as a communication link between domains of the industry. Norwest's best managers kept the team connected both to goals and to each other by continually updating and sharing information.

Managers should only complain upward

Many employees base their confidence in organizational directives and goals on the attitudes of their managers, emphasizing the importance of managers displaying a positive outlook. Ewing Kauffman, founder and chairman of the board of Marion Laboratories, advises, "Don't ever complain sideways or downward—it destroys morale. If you have a complaint, take it upward to your boss or up to the top if necessary" (Walton, 1989, p. 59).

Bartolome (1993) points out, "Decline of information flow is often a first sign of trouble...subordinates communicate less, express opinions reluctantly, avoid discussions, even meetings" (p. 11). An effective manager makes a positive contribution to the information flow by keeping staff up to date and informed, explaining decisions and policies, and providing accurate feedback. One manager stated, "If I don't know the answer to a question, I tell my workers I'll find out and get back to them. I make sure that I follow through, even if it's to update them on what I've done."

The importance of a manager as an organizational liaison is captured in Redding's (1972) conclusion, "The better supervisors tend to be more open in passing along information; they favor giving advance notice of impending changes and explaining the reasons behind policies and regulations" (p. 443). Supervisors can help reduce organizational distortion by serving as a resource for reliable and current information.

Developing channels for upward influence

The effectiveness of downward communication with staff is, in part, influenced by perceptions of how much influence a manager has in upward communication. In fact, employees' satisfaction may be influenced by their level of confidence in the manager's ability to influence those higher in the chain of command (Pelz, 1952).

A family counselor described her work with the clinical director at a mental health agency. She explained, "The director overreacts to many daily events. He runs up and down the hall clamoring about a crisis. Because of his style, he has little or no influence on those above him." The counselor summarized, " He's terrified of his own director, which decreases respect for his leadership. We don't believe he can protect his employees." Organizational morale, commitment to goals, and employee cooperation are difficult in this organization, as opposed to one which promotes the perception that its managers are listened to and have influence in the decision-making processes.

Cultivate upward channels

Riley and Eisenberg (1993) characterize the cultivation of upward influence as the process of championing ideas, proposals, and actions on behalf of the staff who work for us. Based on an understanding of the senior manager's needs, Riley and Eisenberg (1993) describe a six-step process for designing persuasive arguments that may influence those higher in the chain of command.

- Plan – Prepare a strategy that demonstrates an understanding of decisions and resources.
- Determine why your boss should bother to listen. Connect the persuasive message to values and goals of the senior managers.
- Tailor your arguments to the manager's style and characteristics. Adapt the appeal and evidence to a style favored by the boss.
- Assess the boss's prior technical knowledge. Be able to translate jargon and required knowledge into terms the boss will understand.
- Build coalitions. Determine the level of support for ideas elsewhere in the system.
- Present a well-organized and well-articulated proposal. Packaging and selling of the information may be as important as the information that you present. (p. 230)

Facilitating clear understandings of tasks and responsibilities

Differences in perceptions concerning job responsibilities are a major source of frustration in organizations. Employees frequently describe their situation with comments like, "I'm not sure what my job is. It's changed so much," or, "I feel insecure because it's hard to know if I've done enough or done it right." Studies in the health care industry have found that lack of clarity in regard to roles and responsibilities contributes to a closed communication work environment and a work climate in which employees tend to withdraw from the social dimensions of the organization (Albrecht, 1982). Lack of clarity creates an unsettling anxiety in employees.

Managers often fail to spend sufficient time and energy explaining and clarifying how tasks are to be completed. Supervisors often believe they communicate with subordinates more frequently than they actually do, and that their communication is more effective than it actually is. One supervisor confided, "Sometimes we don't explain tasks because we don't know how to do it ourselves." In this case, an ongoing dialogue between supervisor and employee would enhance the possibility that the tasks are completed at least close to expectations.

Inconsistent management messages are frequently linked to rigid priorities with little understanding of how, given the current resources, the goals could be achieved. Bill Chapman, a telecommunications firm manager, advises, "Expectations need to be as clear as possible. The issue is not can they repeat the message back to me, but do they understand the message." There may be a job description on department letterhead, but is there a shared understanding of what the responsibilities mean? Tasks may be enumerated at a staff meeting, but do staff members understand what those tasks involve?

In one weekly staff meeting, a supervisor assigned a task to one of the members of the team. The employee listened appropriately and wrote down the task word for word. Later at lunch she asked another team member, "Do you have any idea what the job is that I was assigned?" As this shows, we must devote effort to creating shared understandings as well as delivery of the message. Perceived agreement with respect to responsibilities makes a significant contribution to both worker and supervisor satisfaction (Lamuda, Daniels, & Graham, 1988). Shared understandings based on negotiated perceptions serve to build ownership for common goals and commitment to organizational tasks necessary to reach the goals.

How to Promote Shared Understanding

- Look for points of agreement before discussing points of disagreement
- When you feel like reacting emotionally, ask at least two questions that probe for further information
- When the discussion moves into polarizing philosophies, reframe it to look at specific immediate concerns
- Listen for a hidden agenda which might be blocking someone's commitment to understanding
- Search for areas in which you might agree in principle before seeking agreement over courses of action

---

Upward communication: Influencing supervisors

Upward communication occurs whenever workers attempt to influence those of higher rank in the organizational hierarchy. The quality and quantity of upward communication depends heavily upon management's receptiveness to influence. Many workers resist speaking to managers out of fear or lack of trust that they will be heard. In a survey of 5200 former health care workers, 75% stated that they had chosen to leave the field because they believed it was unsafe to talk to their managers about issues (Managers, listen, 1987). The most frequently cited areas were possibilities for advancement (67%), perception that pay is unfair (59%), lack of support by the supervisor (57%), and unfair treatment (50%). Workers who have been successful in influencing supervisors, on the other hand, share several common characteristics:

- Engaging in constructive arguing
- Providing reason-based requests
- Editing unconstructive messages
- Creating groundwork for collaborative exchanges
- Speaking as an organizational advocate

Constructive arguing

Many workers stereotype supervisors as wanting "yes" men and women who will not "rock-the-boat." Because of this stereotype, workers often adopt a passive style when discordant information is passed down. In an effort to avoid conflict, they don't give any negative feedback. This may be an effective strategy in some situations. But in a study of 146 supervisors from a variety of corporate settings, Kent State University professors Dominic Infante and William Gorden (1989) found that many supervisors valued something different. They were most satisfied with workers who demonstrated argumentativeness yet were not verbally aggressive. In other words, supervisors want employees who focus on the issues and the rationales rather than personalities. Workers who couple argumentativeness with antagonism, blaming, and complaining are viewed as having less influence. However, those who argue constructively were perceived by managers as "friendly, relaxed, and attentive communicators, lacking in verbal aggressiveness" (Infante & Gorden, 1989, p. 87). Constructive messages were enhanced by the communicator's ability to be precise, animated, and open to response.

Dialogue on decisions

Sue Baker, a software engineer for MCI, affirms the importance of constructive arguing in her assessment, "I think you should be straightforward in communication with supervisors. I don't believe in beating around the bush. Don't sound like you are making up their minds for them, but communicate that you want to dialogue about decisions."

Influencing supervisors requires avoiding statements that tell them what to do and focusing on dialogue concerning the best course of action. Sharing opinions on information, tasks, and goals helps encourage greater productivity.

Reason-based requests

Effective upward influence is more likely when their is willingness to explain the "why" of messages. Keys and Case (1990) found that providing analysis that supports conclusions and using an explanation of the rationale were among the most effective tactics for influencing managers of higher rank. Peter Garcia, Lieutenant of Police for City and County of Denver's 1000-member police force, rates "use of reasons" as the most important factor in upward influence. He states, "If workers have a request, they should include specific justification. Explain how it will enhance the workers' jobs, or help them complete their assignments more effectively."

Mary Colton, fitness specialist and staff supervisor for a Denver recreation center, shares a similar theme. "Don't just repeat details to me. Tell me why things happen. Justify the way you want things done. Make it clear to me. You gain credibility when you give me reasons." Messages that are grounded in reasons and rationale stand a greater chance of being taken seriously. Managers want to know how your concerns or requests help them as well as the workers.

Show the benefits

Nadia Younes, Human Resource Manager, links reasons to the needs of the organization in her assessment, "I need to prove to my supervisors that my request benefits them. I have to show them how it contributes to the bottom line of the organization. If I can't justify it, I'm not going to get leader sponsorship necessary for my programs to be successful. The people above me drive it as much as the staff below me."

Reasoning that, in some way, addresses organizational values also may enhance the receptivity of managers. For example, a reason-based request might be in the form, "I'd like to request that you give my idea further consideration. I think it will help us be more competitive with clients," or "Going to this training seminar will improve my performance in the customer service area. I believe that the skills I'll learn will be useful in all areas of our outreach."

University professors Rudolph and Kathleen Verderber (1995) propose three criteria that should be met when we use reasons as a tool for influencing supervisors:

1. The reason should be more than superficial and should genu inely support the idea or request.
2. The reason should be supportable by further explanations or presentation of facts.
3. There should be a good likelihood that the person you are attempting to influence is open to reason. (p. 268-269)

Providing reasons for our thinking sets us apart from others who state firm opinions without rationale for them. Providing reasons communicates that we are reasonable and open to dialogue. It supports a perception that we want what is best for both our supervisor and the organization for which we work.

Editing unconstructive messages

The *way* we say something can have a greater impact on reception of the message than *what* we say. Some messages push other people away instead of getting action. Consider the following types of messages:

- Scolding: How could you have possibly done things that way?
- Judging: You don't know how to manage people.
- Demeaning: You just don't get it, do you?
- Blaming: It's your fault this happened.

We may believe that we are instructing someone out of our greater wisdom, but we are actually facilitating defensiveness and emotional distance. Using unconstructive messages or a negative tone of voice often has greater risk than reward.

For example, consider the emotional climate created by the following employee, Barb. Barb has a high standard for her work and high respect for organizational goals. Barb works at a fast pace and provides high quality output. However, under stress, she speaks bluntly without regard for the feelings of colleagues. Recently, she said to her supervisor, "There's a vacuum of leadership around here. We need clearer direction." At a meeting of the whole staff, she said, "With a faster response from leadership, we could've had this project completed weeks ago!" Barb's supervisor has no doubt about where the criticism is directed. Though Barb's goal is positive, the impact of her message is negative. Her supervisor's response is not, "Thank you for the great input," it is, "Get with the program or get out!"

University of Kentucky communication professor Vincent Waldron (1991) asked 117 non-supervisory workers from manufacturing and service organizations to identify tactics they used to influence supervisors.

The questionnaire provided a list of over 100 descriptions of how to talk to organizational superiors. Based on an analysis of the impact of the tactics, Waldron concluded that workers who successfully influenced supervisors "apparently invest considerable communicative effort to edit messages, avoid negative exchanges, and generally minimize relational problems" (p. 301). Based on the results of the study, he suggests we edit any messages that might do the following:

- Embarrass the manager
- Suggest you can't take feedback or criticism
- Escalate unconstructive conflict
- Convey lack of commitment to agreements that have already been made
- Display a negative attitude when you have been asked to do Something
- Display rudeness or disrespect

Creating groundwork for collaborative exchanges

Influencing managers requires a series of communication behaviors that contribute to meeting the stresses and challenges of organizational life. Workers who appear to have a solid foundation for collaborative exchanges with managers recommend the following actions:

- Display a receptive attitude
- Let the manager know how you are trying to meet expectations
- Don't be bashful about affirming the manager
- Look for opportunities to talk informally with the manager
- Communicate in a way that allows the manager to preserve self-respect

Validate and respect superiors

Employees at all levels tend to relate better with people who validate and respect them. Managers are no different in this regard. For example, Jennifer is an executive assistant in a computer firm. She prepared an extensive report which her manager, Sally, was to present to a monthly meeting of directors. It had been a bad day for Sally, and she arrived at the meeting without the report. When it was her time to speak, Sally panicked because she had forgotten the report. Jennifer immediately jumped up and said, "Oh, I'm so sorry. I left the report on the desk. Let me step out for a moment and get it." By her simple action, Jennifer helped her manager avoid embarrassment which would have added to her already stressful day.

In a fast-paced work environment, we value those people who provide support for us and help us look better on the job. National organizational consultant Kare Anderson (1993) recommends that workers invest energy in helping others preserve self-respect. She says,

> *Find something to like or respect about the other person and speak to that issue...Never embarrass or humiliate others, regardless of how upset you get. Safeguard the relationship, even if at the moment, you never want to see that person again. You will either gain an ally or avoid making an enemy. (p. 176-177)*

We may believe that our wisdom is better than management's, but to have our ideas heard, we must prepare a foundation for sharing it. Try to follow the rule of affirming in public and withholding criticism for private discussions. For example, in staff meetings, don't discuss controversial issues that might make someone (especially the manager) look bad. Save them for closed-door conversations. Harris (1993) advises,

> *Disagreeing with your supervisor should only be over significant issues, and subordinates must have the capability of backing off if the issue seems important to the boss. If objectives appear to be penny-ante, the subordinate is perceived as an irritant and not a 'team player.' (p. 317)*

Waldron (1991) found that showing commitment to a manager's expectations contributed to an employee's ability to influence by conveying that the worker is a "team player" and working with, not against the manager. Ways to do this include:

- Ask the manager for work-related advice
- Let the manager know that you are following his or her suggestions
- Clarify the manager's perceptions concerning your responsibili ties
- Express compliance to rules the manager has established

Organizational advocacy

A health care manager describes what she termed "the towel dispenser crisis." One of her staff members provided counseling services in an office that shared an adjoining wall with a restroom. On the back of the restroom wall was a lever-operated towel dispenser that made a loud clanging sound whenever it was used. The counselor became irritated with the noise of the towel dispenser intruding during her counseling sessions. She complained about the constant interruption, but didn't do anything about it. The manager contacted maintenance personnel, who didn't feel they needed to deal with the dispenser since it functioned well where it was. For two years, the counselor complained about how bad conditions were, but she did nothing to remedy the problem. Her complaining about the towel dispenser became one of many wedges between the worker and her manager. One day the manager had enough. She took a screwdriver into the restroom and in minutes had the dispenser moved to the other side of the wall. She put a picture over the holes left by the screws and solved the complaint. The manager later shared, "I want an active employee, someone who promotes ideas on how to improve the business, not complain. I want someone who helps brainstorm solutions."

Workers usually find they have more power influencing managers if they become part of solutions than if they keep pointing at all that is wrong. This requires developing organizational advocacy or "the process of championing ideas, proposals, actions, or people to those above you in the organization" (Eisenberg & Goodall, 1993, p. 230).

Advocacy is part attitude and part proactive communication. It involves communicating constructive perspectives about how problems might be addressed, pointing out what is good about the organization, and promoting ideas that will improve processes. The advocacy approach differs from an attitude that says, "I just do what I'm told. I collect my paycheck and go home." Communication behaviors that demonstrate organizational advocacy include:

- Displaying an attitude of appreciation for organizational goals
- Sharing messages that support or affirm colleagues
- Editing messages that involve unconstructive criticism
- Demonstrating a cooperative attitude, rather than a whining, antagonistic style
- Tailoring messages to the values, needs, and interests of leadership
- Focusing on common ground in discussions rather than on issues that polarize
- Seeking to be part of the solution, not the problem

Workers who champion the goals and needs of the organization usually find greater receptiveness to their ideas and requests. This communication style also creates stronger likelihood of a positive organizational climate, with added benefits in terms of productivity and morale.

Qualities of a Leader

Part I. Rate how strongly you agree with each of the following statements.

1. Leaders should model the competencies or skills that they expect from those who work for them.

5	4	3	2	1
Completely	A great deal	Moderately	Only a little	Not at all

2. Respect is the most important factor in the relationship between manager and worker.

5	4	3	2	1
Completely	A great deal	Moderately	Only a little	Not at all

3. In order to avoid the perception of favoritism and polarization of staff, managers should restrict displays of friendship or closeness with any staff during work hours.

5	4	3	2	1
Completely	A great deal	Moderately	Only a little	Not at all

4. I like a leader who closely follows my work to the point of noting out small details
that I need to improve. I want to know honestly when I'm not meeting standards.

5	4	3	2	1
Completely	A great deal	Moderately	Only a little	Not at all

5. Good managers involve their staff in discussion of all issues for which the department is responsible.

5	4	3	2	1
Completely	A great deal	Moderately	Only a little	Not at all

6. Group morale should be the highest priority of a group leader even if it means going slower on tasks or meeting goals.

5	4	3	2	1
Completely	A great deal	Moderately	Only a little	Not at all

7. Good leaders should learn to accept all feedback from staff, no matter how much it disagrees from their perspective.

5	4	3	2	1
Completely	A great deal	Moderately	Only a little	Not at all

8. The manager and worker have equal responsibility for the worker's career and success in the organization.

5	4	3	2	1
Completely	A great deal	Moderately	Only a little	Not at all

Part II.

Who are the best organizational leaders you have known? What were the characteristics that made them effective?

CHAPTER SIX

Communication with Peers

From the water cooler to the boardroom, workers are constantly interacting with peers. Studies show that the majority of organizational communication occurs between co-workers as opposed to upward or downward communication between supervisors and employees. By definition, a peer includes any co-worker or colleague similar to you in job status who is not part of your hierarchical relationships in the organization. Your peers work at the desk next to yours, but also exist in every other department, other buildings and other company locations. You may have little in common with an employee whose education or job title is far removed from yours, but working within the same organization makes you peers.

Communication skills with peers influences our power and reputation, as well as their perception of our effectiveness and our value within the organization. Age-old advice dictates, "Never burn your bridges, because you may need the road again." Our peers might someday influence decisions on job status or promotions. They may even become our boss, sometimes causing us tremendous embarrassment and humiliation. Our peers influence the flow of information, providing input and guidance to our work, as well as helping us recognize potential sources of conflict or problems within the organization. Effective peer communication can streamline and encourage our work goals and help us be more productive and effective. This type of information comes from cross-functional communication, meaning co-workers who share in the overall tasks and goals of the organization, even though they may work in far removed departments or locations. A second level of peer relationships results from grapevine communication, the casual chatting that occurs routinely between workers. This level may greatly affect power and influence in the organization.

Cross-functional communication

Employees who communicate with peers in other departments as part of their work day depend on cross-functional communication to enhance their productivity and help them accomplish work tasks. It can also be an endless source of frustration if we deal with people who are uncooperative or unavailable when we need something from them. A regional telephone company discovered their sales staff was being forced to sell products such as cellular phones without knowing how they'd been advertised or how they worked. When the sales reps tried to get more information, the marketing and development team indicated they were protecting trade-secrets and couldn't provide any help.

When cross-functional communication breaks down, workers may justify it with comments like, "That's not my job," or "You'll have to talk to someone else." You may not be able to avoid poor communicators in your organization, but improving your own skills can make communication efforts more effective. When rules dictate that we can't talk to certain departments or employees, we need to find informal ways to get around this. Good relationships with peers can help make the system work in spite of rules. In this section, we will discuss five specific skills that enhance effective communication with peers.

Enhancing Cross-Functional Communication

---

1. Communicate understanding of other's perspectives
2. Promote common ground
3. Facilitate collaborative networking
4. Communicate value for others
5. Accept responsibility for productive communication

Perspective taking

People want to know that others hear what they say and that their point of view is respected and valued. Perspective-taking, or understanding how another person sees an issue, is a significant factor in predicting whether people can negotiate differences in perceptions or interests (Kemp & Smith, 1994). Demonstrating in conversation that we understand how another sees the issue creates an emotional climate of greater communication responsiveness, willingness to volunteer, and willingness to share comforting messages that reduce sources of stress (Stiff et al., 1988). People tend to trust and communicate with people they believe understand them. Perspective-taking is perceived as empathetic understanding and often promotes a desire to reciprocate.

What we have here is...
a failure to communicate

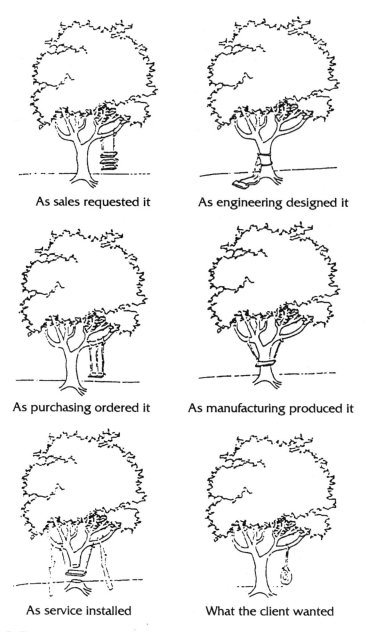

As sales requested it   As engineering designed it

As purchasing ordered it   As manufacturing produced it

As service installed   What the client wanted

Figure 2. Trees

Too often, people approach an issue from a fixed mindset of how they think things should be. As one worker put it, "They can't see the issue from outside of their mental box." This fixed orientation communicates that they are not open to dialogue or to the value of what the other has to offer.

Improving Perspective Taking

Instead of	Try saying
Let me tell you what I think	Let me state what I hear you saying
I've made up my mind	Before I make my decision, would you explain how you see this issue?
You just don't get it do you?	Help me understand what you mean

Perspective-taking does not mean that you agree with the point of view of the other person. However, it demonstrates that you are committed to understanding their message and what it means to them.

Promote common ground

In the past two decades major organizations have shifted to greater specialization in responsibilities. This often limits the opportunity to follow a service or product from development to delivery. We've become more focused on our own specialized areas and less knowledgeable about other areas of expertise. This frequently causes turf-battles in which each person seeks to protect his or her resources. When communicating with peers across department lines, we must strive to explain our interests and fill in the gaps that others may not understand. One manager began every departmental meeting with a ten-minute summary of the previous meeting and resulting actions or changes. When asked why she devoted this much time to summarizing, she explained, "Invariably someone missed the last meeting or was not aware of the actions taken. This quick review puts everyone on the same page and saves repeating everything several times during the meeting time." By creating a shared history and awareness, she was promoting common ground and a more efficient process.

Principles for Promoting Common Ground

- Do not assume that others understand
- When others approach issues from their limited viewpoint, don't get mad or fight it. Instead, share information and help them understand
- Encourage others to stay centered on the present issue. Separate agendas often contribute to non-productive tangential discussions
- Focus on being specific instead of speaking in generalities that obscure meaning

---

Facilitating collaborative networking

Competitiveness drives us to achieve in areas such as education, sports, sales, or the military. In some organizations, it may serve as a motivating factor for promotions and raises. But in communication with peers, competitiveness polarizes and undermines effective communication. The reward for competitiveness may be a brief moment of higher status, or a fragile expression of admiration. But the price is that workers snipe at each other in staff meetings, withhold valuable information from fellow workers, and talk disparagingly about co-workers in the lunch room. Unfortunately, these behaviors create a downward spiral in terms of the quality of the relationship. When the situation gets bad enough, changing personnel often becomes the only remedy for stopping the negative impact on organizational dynamics.

We can overcome the need to compete with peers by investing time in getting to know them better. This collaborative networking becomes vital for accomplishing our goals in the most efficiently manner possible. Amy Blackwell, a national hair styling specialist for American Crew, points out that constructive communication between peers begins with supporting each other with positive feedback. "If you don't say it to them, say it to someone else." In contrast, constantly competing with peers may cause others to distrust us and isolate us in the organization.

Garry Woody, staff industrial engineer for Lockheed-Martin Astronautics, points out that in the aerospace industry there is a lot of interdepartmental rivalry. To manage the competitiveness, he suggests two factors: "First, don't be so critical of what others are doing. Appreciate the good in what they do, and leave it at that. Secondly, stop being afraid that someone else is going to do it better. Learn from others and be less defensive." Being competitive can push us to accomplishments, but it often comes with the high price of shutting down collaboration.

Cooperation vs. competition

In the 1970s, Robert Axelrod hosted a tournament for game theorists. The goal was to create a computer program that produced the best outcomes based on a balance of cooperation and competition. Sixty-three representatives from seven countries submitted entries. The participants came from psychology, economics, political science, mathematics, sociology, physics, and computer science. The tournament was conducted twice and the same formula won both times. The successful approach can be summarized in four steps:

1. Start off being nice. Cooperate as long as possible.
2. Allow yourself to be provoked. You may defend yourself or express your displeasure if the others react competitively.
3. Be forgiving; Otherwise, you'll never get back to cooperation.
4. Be clear about what you're doing. Others need to see reasons behind your choice of actions. (Axelrod, 1984)

One implication of this formula for peer relationships is to begin with cooperation. If the other person competes so that it drives a wedge in the relationship, we should not hesitate to acknowledge the impact competition has on us. At this point, we may choose to protect ourselves, but we must avoid creating a dynamic of retaliation and retribution. When people have been hurt by others, they often believe they can't trust anyone. Overcoming this belief doesn't require blindly trusting everyone as much as determining who to trust with what.

Examples of Promoting Collaboration

- I appreciate the extra effort that you gave me with this project. I know you had lots of other things to do. Your help made my day.
- I am glad you are here. I really value your expertise and willingness to share it with those of us who truly need it.
- Thanks for getting me that information. I hope you'll feel free to call on me when you need something as well.

Ron Adler (1986), a Santa Barbara City College specialist in business communication, recommends that we develop an organizational network of peers with whom we cooperate based on three principles:

1. Seek exposure to people in many levels of the organization
2. Treat everyone within the organization with respect
3. Don't flaunt the informal shortcuts that you develop (p. 39).

In an era of tight budgets and limited resources, organizations will continue to place value on workers who demonstrate collaborative skills. Supporting the work of our peers and developing strong channels of cooperation will benefit our own work status and outcomes.

Communicate value for others

In 1991, researcher Dennis Kinlaw investigated communication in corporations and government agencies. He found that messages that show value for others create a greater potential for positive outcomes, including relationships between members, and the group's ability to cooperate as a team. On quality work teams, workers communicated messages such as, "Nobody was left out," "We respected each other," "People went out of their way to make somebody else look good," and "If someone needed help, we all jumped in" (Kinlaw, 1991, p. 48-50).

Perhaps energy devoted to valuing others is somewhat analogous to a bank account. Each valuing statement serves as a deposit and, in time, brings returns with interest. Each devaluing statement in the form of sarcastic remarks, depreciation of another's skills, or harmful gossip is a withdrawal from the account. In the short term, we don't see much damage caused by devaluing remarks (which we might justify with comments such as, "I was just being honest") but in the long term we pay a great price in terms of credibility, cooperation, and trust.

Janie Chambers, a retail service manager for First Data Corporation, a Fortune 500 Company, points out that in a highly competitive work environment, communicating value to others becomes even more important. She notes, "The corporate atmosphere is behind the times in letting employees know they are important. I want them to tell me how I've contributed. Tell me how I helped the bottom line. Acknowledge me and value my feedback."

As we affirm the positive contributions of others we narrow the distance between workers that occurs naturally in competitive work environments. Communicating value requires a commitment to talking *with* others, not *at* them. A communication style that demonstrates this will include:

- Allowing room for other perspectives
- Avoiding words such as always, never, or impossible, which deny the validity of other viewpoints
- Focusing on what is positive and constructive in another's viewpoint.

Honesty and providing valuing communication can increase our peers' sense of satisfaction with the relationship, and provide greater motivation to meet expectations (Rossiter & Pearce, 1975).

Valuing communication can unconsciously be sabotaged by devaluing nonverbal messages. Facial expressions and body posture may communicate that what others have to contribute is not important and that their presence is not appreciated. The following chart summarizes some of the commonly accepted interpretations of nonverbal messages that occur in American culture.

Nonverbal Message Interpretations

Eye and Facial Messages	Possible Interpretations
Frown	Displeasure, dislike
Smile	Acceptance, friendliness
Raised eyebrows	Disbelief, amazement
Avoiding eye contact	Lack of sincerity, lack of respect, deception
Steady eye contact	Interest, concern, confidence
Intense stare	Display of power

Body Postures and Gestures	Possible Interpretations
Fidgeting, cracking knuckles	Boredom, disinterest, nervousness
Hands on hips	Defensiveness, anger
Shrugging shoulders	Disinterest
Leaning forward	Interest, concern
Leaning away	Boredom, lack of interest
Arms folded	Defensiveness
Finger pointing	Judgment, scolding

A health care worker described her manager's common nonverbal communication, "She rarely makes eye contact, talks with a clenched jaw, and faces away with folded arms. If you're in her office and the phone rings, she'll answer it while you wait. Her actions communicate disrespect, and I assume that she doesn't value me."

Accepting responsibility for productive communication

In many organizations, technical workers believe that they are hired to do a job and not to worry about human relations. They consider interpersonal communication to be nonproductive, and occasionally, a waste of time. In a class for senior executives, a corporate vice president quipped, "I don't have to relate. They do." These attitudes limit producing cooperative communication in work environments. Instead they create a stressful work climate with negative impacts on morale and productivity. Eisenberg and Goodall (1993) point out that, "for many individuals interpersonal communication is the work of the 1990s, particularly among managers" (p. 232).

A worker at a government agency commented, "Why should I bother to work on communication? This organization is too big and my little bit won't make a difference." It's difficult to argue with this reasoning since her efforts may not be able to influence the wider organization; they will, however, be appreciated by her co-workers and her peers at staff meetings. When we adopt the dysfunctional behaviors of the organization, we lose a little of our integrity and sacrifice quality in our relationships. Responsibility for communication begins with us. We can't make the whole world a better place because of our actions, but we can make our immediate world more enjoyable to work in.

In addition, the poor communication behaviors practiced at work also impact relationships outside the work setting. Marriages and families often receive the over-spill of stressful days at work and dysfunctional work relationships. Our emotional health, such as self-esteem, can be harmed by an unhealthy work climate. Virginia Satir, nationally known counseling psychologist, frequently said in her programs, "Peace among the nations of the world begins with the peace I share with others."

Grapevine

In addition to the cross-functional communication network among peers, workers share information that defies all formal boundaries and roles, through the *grapevine*. We are exposed to the grapevine in our earliest moments of orientation for a job. Someone may tell us what it's like to work there, how management operates, or what potential changes might occur all presented off the record. In a study showing the source of employees' organizational information, 55% said their first source was their supervisor while 40% indicated it was informal networks (Manning & Curtis, 1988). When asked, "But what are your preferred sources of information?" Most employees favored the supervisor, while the informal network, the grapevine, dropped to 15th. Although workers participate in the grapevine, they clearly prefer to hear information about the organization from management. Grapevines serve as an integral part of every organization and actually provide several useful functions.

Benefits of the grapevine

- *Story telling*
  Members tell stories that create and save a shared history. These stories serve as legends of the organization and teach values of the culture. "Do you remember when...?"
- *News source*
  News concerning advancement possibilities, raises, organizational change, and the health of the organization often filter down through the grapevine. This news may fill information gaps in the information from the more formal channels. The grapevine also allows information to be accessed by those who normally wouldn't be privileged to hear it. "Tell me what's new around here."
- *Social linking*
  The greatest share of grapevine messages are rumors about people. The act of talking about people or events creates a social fabric for the organizational culture. These stories link people together with common values and concerns. "Have you heard the latest plan? What are we going to do about it?"
- *Sense making*
  Formal channels often provide information without explaining meaning or implications. The grapevine interprets, clarifies, and explains information. This function provides the worker with a sense of control. "Now I understand what's going on."
- *Emotional outlet*
  Workers who do not feel comfortable expressing displeasure with superiors require an outlet for their emotions. The grapevine becomes a relatively safe place to disagree with organizational dynamics. In this sense, the grapevine may become subversive because it creates coalitions and dissension in response to organizational plans. "Let me tell you how I would do it if I were in charge."

Although many would like to abolish grapevine networks, attempts to do so have been unsuccessful. Wherever there are human organizations, there will be informal networks that share stories, catch up on what's new, and react to established authority.

Information can be rapidly disseminated along the grapevine network. In a study of a company with 600 workers, 67 of whom were management, Davis (1988) found that it took about six work hours for information to circulate to 43% of the managers. He also found that only 10-20% of the executives actually transmitted information. Additionally, Davis found that the type of content affected the breadth of transmission. Personal information about managers reached more workers (81%) than information about quality control issues (68%). In terms of accuracy, scholars estimate that the grapevine is correct 75-90% of the time for non-controversial information (Deal & Kennedy, 1982).

Telecommunications manager Bill Chapman suggests that the grapevine, "is a source of information with a probability number attached to it. There are many pieces to the picture. They must all be laid out on the table to get the whole picture." He cites as an example a business in Santa Monica, California, that used a lot of telecommunications equipment. A major earthquake caused a power outage and much of the equipment shut down. A rumor surfaced via the grapevine in the central telecommunication's office that technicians would be asked to go into structurally-damaged condemned buildings to get the equipment up and running. One worker said, "I don't care what the customer wants. We shouldn't have to go into condemned buildings." Then in an angry voice, another worker suggested that the manager call the customer and explain how the workers feel. After a few quick phone calls, the manager put pieces of the picture together. On the day of the earthquake, the customer said to a telecommunications representative, "We *might* ask you to come in and get the system up and going soon." That same day, a television newscast reported that all buildings in Santa Monica were damaged and some may have to be condemned. A telecommunications operator put the two pieces together and delivered a message to the central office, "Our technicians *will be asked* to go into the condemned buildings and get the equipment working." Information had not yet been released on the condition of this specific building or how soon the customer needed the equipment operational. Potential conflict between customer and client was averted by a manager who took time to look critically at the grapevine information. Chapman points out that when dealing with grapevine information, "Question the pronouns such as *he, she, it,* and *they*. Ask who these pronouns refer to so that you can assess the reliability of the information."

Hellweg (1987) identifies the following characteristics of organizational grapevines:

- Five out of six messages in organizations travel through informal channels
- Grapevine rumors include those that express anxiety, those that express wants, and those that polarize workers from each other or management

- Generally, information carried on the informal network is inappropriate for formal channels
- The grapevine tends to become stronger the more secretive an organization becomes
- Participation in the grapevine is not a function of gender
- As organizations grow in size, so does the level of grapevine activity

Because a grapevine occurs wherever humans work in organizations, we need to develop strategies for how to deal with it. Our choice of relationships, who we are able to connect with in the organization, and the placement of our work space, all influence our relationship to the grapevine. Dealing with the grapevine is sometimes difficult because we can do everything correctly and still become the subject of rumors. The following four principles suggest ways to raise the odds that people will treat us fairly in grapevine discussions:

1. Make connections with workers on many levels of the organization
2. Work to achieve centrality
3. Improve chances for reciprocity
4. Volunteer for tasks that provide opportunity to collaborate with others

Make connections on many levels of the organization

Access to knowledge and resources depends on the richness of the informal network that we establish. The more people we relate to, the wider our base of knowledge. Researcher David Krackhardt (1990) looked at the patterns of relationships in a communications firm. He found that people with more communication contacts were perceived as having more influence than would be expected from their job title. Conversations with workers at many levels of the organization provide valuable information concerning work priorities, areas of indifference, and potential conflict. A wide range of contacts informs employees where energy is best invested, and where it is a waste of time. Administrative assistants are often the best sources of information concerning ways to get a project done and where to find resources. Mid-level managers can serve as advance warning systems about politically-sensitive courses of action.

Industrial engineer Garry Woody suggests that workers, especially managers, should, "Tap into the grapevine so that you can understand how people are thinking. In a formal setting, people will say things they're expected to say. The grapevine will tell us what people are really thinking." People will talk about things at the water fountain that they are afraid to say with the manager present. The grapevine provides an excellent opportunity to assess the morale of different levels of an organization, to understand how workers and managers are valued, and what staff members think about changes.

Katharine Grant, past manager of student services at a Denver university, suggests that the grapevine serves as a support system for workers who fear sharing their opinions with managers, "When people aren't receiving support or acknowledgment from supervisors, they turn to other people to get their needs met. Sometimes the grapevine is used to garner support and strength rather than going directly to the manager. In some cases it helps power."

Work to achieve centrality

Achieving centrality begins with physical placement of the office. Jeff Pfeffer (1992), professor of organizational behavior at Stanford University, points out the importance of proximity of a worker's office for forming and sustaining connections. He writes,

> The importance of physical arrangements for inhibiting interaction should never be underestimated. Where one sits has an important effect on the number and content of one's interactions. And this in turn, influences what one knows, whom one knows, and one's relationships with others. (p. 121)

He recommends that workers who want to achieve organizational centrality work toward strategic placement of their offices so that they might be on the communication paths of the organization.

Achieving centrality also requires being visible in organizational meetings and company get-togethers. This runs counter to a cultural trend toward "cocooning." Cocooning is physically withdrawing from social interaction, avoiding get-togethers, staying home with the remote control in hand, screening phone calls, and sheltering ourselves from cultural stresses (Popcorn, 1991). Meetings provide opportunities to form cooperative relationships, while organizational gatherings help to cultivate friendships favorable to the grapevine.

Improve chances for reciprocity

Our reputation on the grapevine is, in part, a reflection of how well people like us. We can give people reasons to like us, which, in turn, improve chances for them to return favors. Affirming others, displaying interest in

what they are doing, being friendly, and doing favors, improve our connection with others. People generally trust and like people who show an
interest in them, while they tend to distrust people they don't know. For
example, Rose (1989) points out that a primary reason for why Steve Jobs
lost his position of leadership in Apple Computer, a company which he co-
founded, was because others viewed him as "self centered and incapable
of viewing the world from anybody else's perspective" (p. 274). It's easier
to pass on an unfavorable rumor about someone who isn't known well or
who is not well liked.

In daily conversations, try to speak well of others in spite of what you've
heard about them. Practice framing the struggles of workers as caused by
times of growing, difficult changes, or problems generated by being
stretched too thin by work demands. People will view us in much the same
manner as they hear us talking about others. The law of reciprocity indicates
that what we do to others on the grapevine will eventually be done to us.

Volunteer for tasks that provide opportunity for collaboration

Volunteering for committees and task forces provide opportunity for networking outside the department. Influence is significantly related to a
employee's centrality in the work flow of the organization. Promoting this
connection involves occasionally getting outside of our normal work assignments and into the flow of organizational decision making. Interdepartmental committees and task forces bring us into greater contact with
significant workers in the informal network. Even helping plan the company picnic can develop relationships that later benefit our influence in
the organization.

As we cultivate our ability to improve communication skills, we
strengthen our efforts by understanding the powerful difference between
cross-functional communication and organizational grapevine. The level
of influence in each area relates directly to our ability to penetrate the networks, both formal and informal. Pfeffer (1989) concludes, "We can say
that power is a function of one's position in the network of communications and social relations, where this position is assessed not only in terms
of structural centrality, but also in terms of the power of the people with
whom one is connected" (p. 111).

Assessing Our Communication Needs

We each bring different interpersonal needs to the communications setting. On each of the following factors, assess yourself along the continuums.

Low need .... High need
for control   for control

Low need .... High need
for belonging/inclusion   for belonging/inclusion

Flexible .... Rigid

Low trust .... High trust

Submissive .... Dominant

As you look over these scales, what are the insights, patterns, or themes that you observe about yourself?

CHAPTER SEVEN

Communication on Teams

Teams are the trend of the nineties. Corporations are increasingly using teams to enhance problem solving and decision making. By definition, a team is a collection of workers operating cooperatively with a shared agenda, striving to achieve common goals. Ideally, a collaborative team operates with a shared leadership and a group identity that motivates members. Strongly collaborative teams generally outperform individuals working alone and feel more responsible for outcomes, sort of a "we did it" approach.

Team communication will vary based on the make-up of the group, the purpose to the team, and the amount of decision power assigned to the team. Four common types of teams in organizations include:

1. *Problem solving teams*
   Occasionally workers are drawn from different departments for the purpose of studying a problem and making recommendations. Decision-making power is usually limited and the team ceases to exist after completing the task.
2. *Cross-functional teams*
   Members are drawn from a variety of areas and departments for the purpose of monitoring work processes. Decision-making powers are greater than problem-solving teams and groups may last for many projects.
3. *Self-directed work teams*
   As the most autonomous of the teams, members possess full responsibility for decisions necessary for day-to-day operations and how they will accomplish the work. Decisions will often include budget, personnel, planning and assessment of their own success.
4. *Project teams*
   These teams generally work within a specific geographic area of the organization, and possess decision-making authority relevant only to completion of a project. They will usually work on a specific task from beginning to end.

A frequent source of frustration for group members is misunderstanding about the kind of team they are expected to be. Team members may assume they have decision-making power when their role may be to simply offer recommendations. Others want to be involved in organizational issues beyond their current project and find their parameters are limited. Effective team communication must begin with a clear definition of the function, expectations, and goals for that specific team.

Collaborative teams

Studies demonstrate that collaborative teams construct better problem-solving strategies (Nemeth & Kwan, 1987), provide a context for greater emotional support for members (Tjosvold, 1993), frequently achieve greater productivity (Johnson & Johnson, 1989), and complete tasks with higher quality (Dumaine, 1989). Hundreds of corporations and manufacturing plants currently function using a project or work team approach, including divisions of Boeing, Caterpillar, General Electric, Procter and Gamble, Aetna Life, Xerox, and Digital Equipment.

Many organizations, with varying levels of success, attempt to transform work groups into teams. A health care director attended a training seminar on utilizing teams and decided to implement the principles with her 12-member department. Her employees were accustomed to being very autonomous, competitive and self-focused. They tended to display low trust for each other, occasional coalitions, minimal problem solving as a group, and a weak level of support for each other. At their next staff meeting, the director announced, "I want to know how we can work together as a team and improve the morale in our department." But instead of offering enthusiastic suggestions, the staff members began blaming each other for the problems, sniping at other members' work patterns, and engaging in bitter, complaining side conversations. The director soon abandoned her efforts to institute her new concept of teamwork.

Organizations operate by established norms, "rules that designate the boundaries of acceptable behavior in the group" (Kreps, 1990, p. 170). In this case, the well-established norms were more powerful than the director's facilitation skills. The director had a desirable goal but lacked effective procedures for achieving the goal. Members either had insufficient incentive to cooperate or lacked adequate interpersonal skills to be supportive of their colleagues. Group norms, which are a complex product of people, procedures, leadership, and tasks, are often resistant to change. Altering these norms requires support from the organizational structure, leadership that facilitates a collaborative climate, and team members committed to, and capable of, teamwork.

Supportive structure

At a series of training sessions on problem solving and decision making at a major regional communications firm, I observed an interesting norm. During our day-long meetings, managers would frequently reach for their cellular phones to call and get permission to talk about certain topics. Though the goal of management was to empower this problem-solving team, the hierarchical structure severely limited their degree of participation. Eisenberg and Goodall (1993) point out that, "for work teams to be effective, management must make a commitment to empowerment. As empowerment increases, work team members begin to take responsibility for continuous improvement of their processes" (p. 283). Empowering managers might encourage input on disciplinary processes or the performance appraisal system, invite better ways to accomplish tasks, or solicit ideas for customer service or quality control. There must be sufficient incentive, reward, and safety in the organizational culture for workers to believe that they can make a difference. Though teams can survive in less than optimal organizational climates, they function best in climates that provide clear roles and accountabilities, support open channels of communication between management and teams, and give clear direction in terms of vision and goals (Larson & LaFasto, 1989).

Influence of team leadership

At a national banking firm, senior managers described successful mid-level managers as "leaders who invested energy into communication that clearly articulated a credible plan for reaching organizational goals." In problem organizations workers often can see the goal but not know how to get there. Norwest's most successful managers said that they were not afraid of negative feedback. They asked questions in order to identify hidden problems that might get in the way of reaching goals. These managers modeled the same level of respect for co-workers that they asked of their employees.

Lawrence and Lorsch (1969) found that the number of collaborative tactics used with work groups was directly correlated to higher levels of performance. Based on a review of studies comparing skills used to manage employee differences, Sashkin and Morris (1986) conclude that, "collaborating is clearly related to positive outcomes in a wide range of circumstances" (p. 327). Larson and LaFasto (1989) found that, "members tend to mirror the collaborative style of the leader" (p. 135).

Work groups frequently complain that decisions are made behind closed doors without employee input. Information is not shared openly, and the option for dialogue is perceived as limited. An oil company employee said, "If we want to find out information, we go to the cafeteria, because our supervisors never tell us what's going on." John Pinelli, Manager of Human

Resources for a communications firm, says that, "effective leaders go to extraordinary efforts to keep the team informed. They constantly give organizational updates or short information announcements which tie the team together. Our leaders are visible, frequently visiting with employees." A team member at a computer firm said, "We do best as a team when leadership gives us a rationale for decisions. I think this makes people believe that they are intrinsically valuable and makes them more committed to the company as a career rather than just a job."

Not all decisions can be made in open settings, but at times, managers may be more secretive than necessary. At Marathon Oil Corporation a frustrated manager told me, "I've had to learn to go to my group members individually and, as hard as it might be, ask what they think and sincerely listen to their answers. I've had to adapt my communication to meet a variety of personalities and needs." He concluded that being open to team members' ideas helped him ultimately make better decisions on employee policies.

Team facilitators

Team leaders often function as facilitators, helping the group "free itself from internal and external obstacles or difficulties so that it may more efficiently and effectively pursue achieving the group's outcomes" (Kayser, 1994, p. 36). With respect to work teams, General Electric CEO Jack Welch believes, "We've got to take out the *boss* element. We're ultimately going to win based on our ideas, not by using whips and chains" (Stewart, 1991, p. 41). Facilitative leaders monitor team disruptive behaviors and keep the group focused on their goals. They also seek out and provide organizational information that enables the group to accomplish tasks, manage meetings so they are not unnecessary time drains on personnel, and promote inclusive, open-minded discussion. Effective leaders know they must balance a group's need for clarity and structure with individual needs for autonomy and control of processes. When leaders overstructure or overcontrol, they create frustration in group members and contribute to ineffective group efforts (Maier, 1967).

Encouraging and sharing facilitative responsibility helps employees feel involved in the team efforts between group members. One department rotated the responsibility of team facilitator, increasing individual participation in the department's responsibilities. Another manager had the team evaluate the group's tasks, and assign responsibility for completion of the task to the members with the greatest knowledge of the subject. This strategy requires facilitators to be very clear in disseminating information prior to deadlines, as well as clarifying task needs and desired outcomes. After reviewing quantitative studies on the organizational leadership of corporate executives, Bolman and Deal (1991) concluded that effective leaders helped establish and communicate a vision, set standards for performance, and provided direction and focus for organizational efforts.

Being an effective team member

A group of workers does not make a team. The success of a team process is influenced by organizational support and the team leadership. But individual members can contribute to the team effectiveness by developing the characteristics that encourage team efforts.

Characteristics of Effective Team Members

- Communicate a strong commitment to team goals
- Suspend criticism in order to support team decisions
- Minimize rigid thinking
- Provide support and validation for team members
- Share responsibility for discussions and decision making in team meetings

---

Commitment to team goals

Collaborative team members communicate a commitment to team goals, even if this means briefly suspending movement toward their personal goals. In a survey of 100 companies on *Fortune's* 1987 list of most admired corporations, respondents ranked "commitment to team goals" as the number one attribute of effective team members (Parker, 1991, p. 71). This requires reviewing objectives and goals as part of discussion processes, and asking questions such as, "What are we hoping to accomplish here?" "Remind me of the goals we began with?" or, "How will this help us get where we want to be?"

Suspend criticism

Effective team members, once a decision is made, strive to suspend personal criticism in order to support team decisions. They demonstrate a willingness to suppress negative comments about the group, the organization, and colleagues in favor of supportive unity. Team members lose credibility when they don't support team agreements or put down a colleague because things didn't go their way. Telecommunication's manager Bill Chapman says that his managers must be in sync with the team, "This means that once we've decided on a course of action as a group, you don't second guess or undermine the decision we've made." Even though they may disagree with choices their group makes, collaborative team members work with the group, not against it.

A consultant was hired to conduct a two-month training series on teamwork for a major government organization. Two days before the training was scheduled to begin, the employees were informed there would be a major downsizing within the year. In spite of the announcement, nearly 65% of the employees participated in the training sessions even though their work schedules had intensified. At the end of the sessions, the director was asked how he would decide which personnel would be laid off. He said, "Generally, their names will be selected from the pool of those who did not attend the team training. They apparently don't want to support team goals and work with our team."

In a list of preconditions for building a team, Patton (1981) includes "commitment to fulfill mutual objectives" and being "committed to the idea that working together as a group leads to effective decisions" (p. 15). In other words, team members need to believe that the group approach is effective for accomplishing tasks. Credibility on teams is directly related to dedication and commitment to group efforts.

Team players also must have the courage to ask "how" and "why" and to work with the team in finding the best answers to these questions. A senior manager of an organization, explained why teams are frequently uncollaborative, "The members are batting for turf and ego." These two factors explain why problem solving and teamwork become difficult at group meetings. If we are to be effective collaborators, we must redirect energy from guarding our turf or building up our egos to developing and supporting group efforts.

Minimize rigid thinking

The third factor that distinguishes effective team members is the ability to minimize rigid thinking and approach discussions with a spirit of humility. Collaborative team members are willing to admit they don't have all the answers, and are willing to engage in a search for the best information or alternatives. More than 200 years ago, Benjamin Franklin spoke to his colleagues at the 1787 Constitutional Convention. He shared his insights concerning the team that was putting together a constitution for a new nation. A common theme in Franklin's message was humility and openness to other perspectives in the decision making process:

Having lived long, I have experienced many instances of being obliged by better information, or fuller consideration, to change opinions even on important subjects, which I once thought right, but found to be otherwise. It is therefore that the older I grow, the more apt I am to doubt my own judgment, and to pay more respect to the judgment of others. (Bolman & Deal, 1991, p. 149)

An employee who was unhappy with the leadership on her team said, "If there's negative feedback, the supervisor will either slam you in front of everybody or railroad right over you. She has great technical knowledge, but she doesn't consider the perspective of others. We've learned to leave her out of the loop." Inability to foster humility and to listen to feedback has cost this supervisor the respect of her employees and the ability to have dialogue with them about essential corporate issues. Floyd Whellan, vice president of human resources for the newspaper and television conglomerate Lee Enterprises, describes the effective team member as someone who "recognizes the importance of having ideas contributed from various sources and is willing to have an 'open window' and permit those ideas to impact their behavior" (Parker, 1991, p. 73).

In a study that compared individual versus group judgments on difficult or complex tasks, Hill (1982) found that groups include a greater range of information and make more accurate decisions than individuals working alone. Refusal to accept information that differs from our perspective is a powerful deterrent to teamwork.

Provide verbal support

A fourth quality demonstrated by effective team members is willingness to communicate verbal support for other team members. This means a willingness to make others look good and contribute to that effort. In the Larson (1995) review of 100 team studies, one of the top four factors that distinguished effective team members from ineffective ones was the ability to support and stand up for other members of the team. Effective members make it emotionally safe for others to contribute without a fear of being unfairly criticized. These workers commit themselves to bringing the best qualities out of all group members through verbal validation and demonstrations of understanding instead of negative evaluation. Fair-weather team members tend to emphasize self-importance and to support team efforts only when it is politically popular.

Share responsibility for group processes

A fifth quality that distinguishes effective team members is their willingness to share responsibility for group processes. Making healthy contributions to group discussions plays a significant role in monitoring group processes. These members help the team to stay on track for accomplishing team goals. In contrast, ineffective team members say, "You're not doing it my way, so I'm saying nothing," or, "If there's nothing in it for me, I'm not going to help." Most of us have been in groups where one member remains silent during group discussions, but later shares information that would have been valuable in the group's deliberations. We generally respond with, "Why didn't you say that the other day to the group?" In contrast, an invested-group member serves as a co-facilitator, sharing and inviting cooperative team efforts.

Ways to Facilitate Effective Group Processes

- Be willing to risk by sharing information and expanding discussion into relevant issues that otherwise might be overlooked.
- Facilitate inclusiveness. Solicit opinions of members who have not been contributing.
- Demonstrate solidarity by supporting and encouraging team members when they make contributions.
- Point out what the group shares in common on an issue before focusing on where there are differences.
- Ask questions that test reasoning, quality of evidence, and implications.
- Encourage the group to look at issues from many perspectives. Promote the concept that every relevant idea should get a fair hearing.
- When the group appears stuck, summarize the previousdiscussions.
- Clarify information that is unclear.
- Bring the group back to the issue at hand if the group members stray too far.
- When the team polarizes, break the problem into more manageable issues or look for common ground between opposing viewpoints.

Team communication at meetings

All of us have had times when we left meetings saying, "That was a waste of time." Both managers and team members should contribute to making meetings constructive and productive. Effective leaders make sure there's a consensus on the purpose for the meeting, as well as an agenda that supports the goals of the group.

Team members come to meetings with different expectations, a variety of work demands, and multiple perspectives concerning priorities. Dan Johnson, an engineering project manager for the Amana Corporation's microwave division says, "Employees are busy and if I don't get to some of their needs quickly, they'll leave. If they think the meeting will go too long, they won't show up. So I have to keep my priorities straight." Johnson identifies the seven principles that help him conduct effective meetings with work teams.

1. *Be sure that all members understand goals for the meeting.*
2. *Respect each member's area of expertise.*
3. *Seek other's perspectives and communicate your understanding.*
4. *When things don't go your way, don't put down team members. Leave an opening that helps them save face.*
5. *Keep people informed before the meeting. Be sure members have the most current information. The more time we have to spend review ing the issues, the less problem solving time is available.*
6. *Anticipate before a meeting how you can be a buffer for members who bring problem issues. If possible, try to negotiate with them before the meeting, or talk with others about effective responses before the issues are brought up in the meeting.*
7. *Be aware that some members don't understand the issues. Train them before or after the meeting concerning the procedures or information they don't understand.*

Seers, Petty, and Cashman (1995) looked at the communication of 103 manufacturing employees who served on work teams. Their research examined the quality of responses with respect to assisting other team members, contribution of ideas, use of feedback, and recognition of other team members. They concluded that *reciprocal behavior* or responsiveness to other members was a significant factor in facilitating group effectiveness and cohesiveness. "The other members should realize that the appreciation, respect, and status of esteemed group members is linked to the contributions they make. Teaching team members to develop their reciprocal exchange relationships may prove an invaluable key to the practical success of teams" (Seers et al., 1995, 36).

Respect my pseudopods

Another way to understand team members involves recognizing how we develop *pseudopods* in our lives. When an amoebae wants to ingest a particle from its environment, it extends its membrane in a kind of false arm, a pseudopod, to engulf and draw in the particle. Social psychologist Ernest Becker (1971) describes the human personality as engaging in symbolic extensions or pseudopods, when it links identity and self-esteem to things valued in the environment. For example, a man may choose to know everything there is about antique cars. He draws esteem from others who appreciate his knowledge about the old cars. This knowledge serves as a pseudopod, an extension of his intellect that he values and wants valued by others. Suppose I said to this gentlemen, "I think the old cars are junk. Nothing good in cars occurred until the 1990s," my comments would serve as criticism for both the antique cars and this man's identity. We all know how our self-esteem can suffer on a bad hair day. On some days our appearance serves as a pseudopod, and when others affirm our manner of dress, our hair, or other aspects of appearance, it will usually boost our self-esteem.

Awareness of pseudopods helps us demonstrate respect and support for others. A colleague recently said, "I've spent six years developing my business. It's a reflection of my identity. In fact, sometimes I get mixed up and think it is my identity." Because her business serves as a pseudopod for her identity, criticizing the business might have a negative impact on our relationship. In organizational settings, pseudopods can include professional competence, status in the organization, loyalty to the corporation, or commitment to hard work. Discovering and respecting the pseudopods of our colleagues is an important step for promoting supportive relationships and constructive dialogue.

In our work with groups, we've identified a team member continuum that extends from energy drainers to energy providers. The following diagram summarizes this principle.

Energy drainer - - - - - Energy neutral - - - - - Energy provider

---

Wears out group	Builds up group
Facilitates tangential discussions	Stays issue focused
Inhibits problem solving	Focuses on problem solving
Has positional orientation	Is needs, goal, interest focused
Promotes coalitions	Promotes consensus
Withholds information for power	Provides information to help

Energy *providers* build up team members through verbal expressions of encouragement, a positive and enthusiastic style, and repeated efforts to remove stumbling blocks. Energizers prefer to try something that falls within the parameters of acceptable risk rather than to be stuck on unproductive paths. Energy *drainers* wear out team members by polarizing the group around positions, personal attacks on member credibility, and tangential discussions that slow problem solving processes to a standstill. Drainers prefer to do nothing in order to avoid failure. With energy drainers we hear, "We can't because...," but with energy providers we hear, "We'll find a way."

Trustworthiness

The effectiveness of a work team is also influenced by the level of trust between two members. Predictability and dependability are two important factors that build trust in work relationships. Lisa Hughes, a project administrator in a 600-member computer consulting firm, reflects these themes in her observation that, "Our effective team members use their expertise to support each other. Team members pitch in to help others meet deadlines without expecting to get credit for it." In groups with a high level of trust, members feel confident that they can talk openly without retaliation. Members help each other discover ways to overcome obstacles.

Hughes also emphasizes the importance of direct one-to-one feedback with another observation: "I would like others to come straight to me if they have a problem with something I've done." Trustworthiness includes a component of giving a group member a chance to explain before taking problems to someone else and making the group member look bad. As a colleague recently shared, "It really burns me when someone who has a problem with my department goes around me and talks to my supervisor."

Research on small groups has demonstrated that when trust is low, group performance diminishes, communication distortions occur, verbal fluency decreases, and interactions become more tense or inflexible. Group members tend to hold back communication from those who have hidden agendas or a history of manipulating people with the information they possess. Trustworthiness begins with modeling dependable, affirming, and predicable communication, "I can count on you not to reject me or put me down to others if I'm honest with you."

Organizational culture impacts teams

A manufacturing firm asked for help in resolving conflict between their major work groups. The organizational structure included a 15-member administration department, a ten-member research department, and 40-

member project team. Administration negotiated the contracts, the research group used state-of-the-art techniques to determine the best direction for the contract needs, and the project team carried out the work required for completion. Relationships and communication between the groups was frequently strained, resentful, and even angry.

The project group complained that administration was inefficient, non-responsive, and slow in obtaining contracts. Some project group members disliked the administration director, and felt their needs were not heard or addressed. One member said, "Administration has no idea how much we do or how we go about it." Others were frustrated with the research team working in isolation without asking for input on current project needs.

The research team characterized the project group as spoiled complainers who would never be satisfied. One member added, "The project group has always felt like an orphan because research and administration work together so closely."

Administration expressed frustration with both groups for not understanding the financial implications of their slow work patterns. The director said, "No one ever grasps the sense of urgency required to get these contracts accomplished on time." All three groups described the communication between teams as highly tense and unconstructive. Each group was convinced that the other departments received more resources than their team. At times the distrust and frustration filtered out within the work groups, decreasing cohesiveness and productivity even further.

As we began studying this organization and conducting interviews to determine the cause of the communication problems, we discovered a fascinating theme. Over the last 20 years the company was known for having personnel problems including distrust, back-biting, and destructive communication between the groups. Developed over many years, this organizational culture served as a lens through which the employees viewed their work setting. The present dilemma resulted from a long history of competition, biased perceptions, and non-cooperation.

Attempting to help this group make constructive changes was constantly challenged by the long-standing organizational climate. Working with this group was like enthusiastically hooking a chain to a chunk of ice to pull it to shore, but then realizing that it was part of a huge iceberg that was hidden in the water. Beneath the initial frustrations of these work teams was an iceberg of hidden agendas, preconceived ideas, and dysfunctional corporate history.

An entirely different culture exists in another manufacturing organization. This 10-year-old company began with a healthy team orientation toward their goals. One supervisor said, "We operate as a team that communicates openly and supportively. We know of no other way. We only hire people who you can work cooperatively on teams." The company expects that all leaders and team members will collaborate in sharing information, problem solving, and coming to the aid of fellow workers.

What do you do with an organizational culture that frustrates the communication efforts of individuals and teams? In reality, you probably can't influence the long-standing cultural norms of the organization. But you can develop your own communication skills to a stronger level and model effective behaviors to others on your team. Even though the organization remains unhealthy, you will be more confident and effective in accomplishing your work goals. Some of your actions may eventually effect changes that will move upward and constructively influence those who define the organizational style.

Ways to influence organizational culture

1. *Use the values that drive the culture*
   If profit is the motivating value, then couple your recommendations with the goal of producing greater profit. Organizations make decisions based on values such as growth, image, success, and productivity. Identify your organization's prominent values and frame your reasoning around these values. A communications firm conducted a major planning symposium to assess development of a new product. For most of the day technicians hammered away at the need to invest millions of dollars and corporate resources into the new product design. After hours of frustrating arguments, the director of marketing said, "You know we're forgetting one thing here, the customer. Our surveys say the customer doesn't want this yet." If the customer doesn't want it, why develop it? A hush came over the room. Then discussion changed, turning to how product development could be integrated better with marketing priorities. The pivotal value that changed the dynamics was identification of the customer's need being the prime value that drove corporate vision.

2. *Break the attribution patterns*
   Attribution theory teaches that people form impressions based on what they see and how they relate it to the past. We pay attention to some aspects of a situation to support our past experiences and ignore issues that disagree with those judgments. Thus we support past stereotypes of people or situations even though we don't know much about the current situation. This pattern causes us to misjudge people's motives or ignore the possibility that maybe something new could be happening in this situation. We can easily conclude, "You see. That's how they are."

   As a teenager, Mike would borrow the car to go to the library. His parents were always convinced that he was out "cruising" because they believed that's what all kids do. No amount of protest would convince them that he really was at the library, often creating some tense discussions after he returned home. We frequently use a preconceived judgment from the past, and assume the present follows the same patterns. This tendency requires less effort than learning about other possibilities and altering our thinking to match them.

We make communication-inhibiting attributions in work settings all the time. Senior management, supervisors, some departments, team members all receive our stereotyped judgments long before they do anything to earn them. To change an organizational culture, even within our department, we need to stop this attribution pattern from inhibiting new possibilities. Otherwise we perpetuate self fulfilling prophecies. The communication breakdown is going to happen because that's exactly what we're expecting. Look for the positive potential in people and events as a first step.

3. *Get small commitments when you can't get big agreements.*
In organizational cultures where there are many roadblocks for effective communication and teamwork, sometimes it's enough to get commitments for minor changes rather than to expect a major overhaul. In groups where nothing seems to work, I will occasionally ask, "Can you just give a little on this one? Just give me this much." I would rather have many small victories than spend all of my time getting worn out trying to win big battles. Create "do-ables" for people as stepping stones on the path toward the way you'd like things to be.

4. *Explore underlying concerns*
We often perpetuate negative organizational culture by jumping to conclusions too quickly. We ask "What's wrong with me?" or say, "This place is nuts" before we have all the information. We need to explore further before casting our permanent judgments. A consultant described the following episode:

> *I was once asked to conduct training at a West Coast organization, and was assigned to work for the manger for two weeks. The goal was to improve employee morale and work with conflict issues. When I arrived, the manager was out of town on a two-day vacation. His assistant directed me to an office across the hall from the department. I settled in with my books and materials and made it a temporary home. When the manager returned from vacation, he immediately called me into his office. He said, "What are you doing in that office across the hall?" I attempted to explain but was cut off. He firmly said, "You don't belong there. Get your stuff out of there. You have no right to just take that office." He ended the scolding*

with, "I'll decide what to do with you later. Let's talk this afternoon." I was ready to get on a plane and go home and forget the entire project.

As I left, I noticed that the manager's staff looked equally stressed. I suspected there was more going on than met the eye. When I returned that afternoon, I began the second meeting with questions about how I have not met the manager's expectations. He first explained that I had misspelled his Irish name on a letter verifying my arrival. I probed further and found out how he dearly valued his heritage and wanted it respected. Next he explained that earlier in the year a supervisor had been very harsh with him for using those offices. Finally, he revealed that the last trainer who had come had been unresponsive to his guidance on how to best work in the organization, and he was worried this would go the same way. I began by apologizing for taking the office, (an apology goes a long way in repairing perceptions) and then asked I could best enhance the work the manager was trying to accomplish in the organization. He looked relieved and responded, "I can see you understand." During the next two weeks, he gave me complete freedom in the organization and supported all of my efforts.

Many times we can defuse potential conflict or misunderstanding by exploring underlying concerns. To achieve this, state clearly that you want to understand, then use effective, focused questions to identify the less visible issues that lie behind the tense messages you receive.

5. Depersonalize organizational dynamics

Poor morale and low self-esteem often result when an organization struggles with negative communication patterns. A nurse who kept trying to initiate changes in her work setting became frustrated with an unsupportive supervisor. For awhile she assumed that her ideas were not creative and that she was not going to accomplish any changes. Then she transferred to another hospital where her ideas were greeted with enthusiasm and changes began to happen as a result.

Poor self-esteem and low self-confidence are often related to a dysfunctional organizational culture rather than a weakness in the employee's personality. A stressful communication climate eventually translates into health problems for employees. For both our mental and physical health, we have to recognize that, "It's not me" and to realize how much the organization affects how we perceive our capabilities. When the culture is stressful, we have to de-personalize the messages.

You can conquer the low self-esteem trap caused by negative organizational cultures by focusing on positive themes in your self-talk. Here are a few ideas:

> I will not allow this to spoil my day.
>
> Will this matter five years from now?
>
> They'll be this way long after I'm gone.
>
> I'm competent and skilled in spite of what I see here.
>
> It doesn't all depend on me, so I'll just do what I can do.
>
> I'll leave work at work when I leave for the day.

Recognize what you can't change

A 70-year-old gentleman was very frustrated with the payment policies for his health care benefits. He said, "If it's the last thing I do, it will be to change how Medicare does its claim procedures." In reality this is the last thing he'll *try* to do, since changing an entire system would be a colossal and probably impossible undertaking. When we decide to take on hospital or school administrations, corporate management, or even our division, we may be naive in thinking we can change a whole system. Grandiose expectations sometimes extend into trying to change clients, our supervisor, or our own family members. When you attempt to influence structures and people over whom you have little power, you become frustrated with your lack of power. We need to recognize areas we can't change and instead focus on situations or people where we have impact. Sometimes you greatly decrease your frustration with your organizational culture by a simple reminder: "You can't change Medicare!"

Assessment of a Work Team

1. How often is friendliness, humor, and warmth shared in your group?

5	4	3	2	1
Most of the time	Often	Moderately	Occasionally	Rarely

2. To what extent do you feel included in the group?

5	4	3	2	1
Completely	A great deal	Moderately	Only a little	Almost none

3. How well do members listen to each other when ideas are shared?

5	4	3	2	1
Outstanding	Good	Moderately	Poor	Very poor

4. When discussing issues, how clear is your group with respect to its goals or purpose?

5	4	3	2	1
Completely	Fairly clear	Moderately	Somewhat unclear	Unclear

5. How are differences of opinion and conflict handled within the team?

5	4	3	2	1
Faced honestly constructively	Talk about most things	Depends on the topic	We manage poorly	Avoidance counterproductive

6. When planning, decision making, or problem solving, direction is largely determined by

5	4	3	2	1
Full group participation	Most of the group	About half the group	Clique	One or two members

7. How often do team members speak well of each other to people outside the group?

5	4	3	2	1
Most of the time	Often	Moderately	Occasionally	Rarely

8. How effective is this team in completing the tasks for which it is responsible?

5	4	3	2	1
Outstanding	Good	Moderately	Poor	Very poor

9. How often do group members set aside their own personal agendas in order to focus on team agenda?

5	4	3	2	1
Most of the time	Often	Moderately	Occasionally	Rarely

10. Once consensus has been reached and group members leave the room, how often are members who had objections willing now to withhold further criticism and support the team?

5	4	3	2	1
Most of the time	Often	Moderately	Occasionally	Rarely

Scores of 20 or below indicate a group that is emotionally unsafe, composed of members who compete with one another rather than cooperate, and that fails to full achieve the group's potential. A score of 21-35 describes a group that gets tasks completed thanks to the hard work of many of the group's members. The group will be productive until the key people who hold it all together leave. A score of 36-50 indicates a healthy group that is adapting, self correcting, and support of member growth. On some projects the results will exceed what anyone initially would have expected.

CHAPTER EIGHT

Communication with Crazymakers

Rarely is it advisable to meet prejudice and passion head on. Instead, it is best to appear to conform to them in order to gain time to combat them. One must know how to sail with a contrary wind and to tack until one meets a wind in the right direction.

Fortune de Felice, 1778

For the last five years, Judith has worked as a manager for a prestigious stock brokerage firm. Judith's boss is a hard-driving woman who worked her way up through the ranks, partly due to her strong skills with understanding and advising complicated stock portfolios. Judith works hard to please her, staying late many nights, and occasionally working weekends. Her boss doesn't plan ahead very well, and will frequently load Judith with extra work on Friday afternoon. When she stretches her schedule to accommodate the work needs, she desperately hopes for some positive feedback. Instead she usually hears comments like, "Why haven't you started the new project yet?"

Judith's boss often makes difficult requests and then reacts in anger when Judith protests. Very particular on how work should be done, the boss will complain about the style of a report and never acknowledge the high quality of the content. When Judith voices concerns, she hears comments like, "You know there are lots of people waiting in line for a job like yours." When Judith's three-person clerical staff suggested they would like more to do on slow days, Judith created a plan for having them manage files for other brokers. When she suggested her idea to the boss, the response was, "If they're not busy enough, we must have too much staff, so I want you to lay one of them off."

Judith says, "I can't seem to please her or do anything right no matter how hard I try. What's wrong with me? What am I doing wrong? I used to think I was a competent professional manager but lately I'm so discouraged that I'm considering leaving the profession."

The problem is not Judith. The problem is that her boss is a crazymaker. She's the kind of difficult person who makes us think we're going crazy or that something is wrong with us, often contributing to making us sick or prone to overeating or too much drinking. Around crazymakers, we feel discomfirmed, invalidated, unsettled and anxious. Our self-esteem suffers, we question our skills and we complain about being very stressed. Hard as we try, we can't seem to avoid conflict—can't please them no matter what we do. They seem to change their emphasis so often that we are never sure of what's important. They point out small typos and never mention getting the big contract or completing a project by the deadline. They are often disorganized and inefficient and as a result, constantly operate in crisis, with us carrying the stress of their intense and unrealistic expectations. In a word: they drive us crazy.

Difficult people who are crazymakers

Bach & Dautsch (1979) use the term *crazymakers* to define a specific group of people who distress relationships and contribute to constant problems with communication. Crazymakers break down the fundamental trust between people, triggering anxiety and confusion, and creating obstacles to smooth interactions. These difficult people show up everywhere, frequently being a significant source of stress in our lives.

A student recently described his efforts to please his crazymaker-style mother:

A few years ago I decided to play the good son role so I called my mother to wish her a happy birthday. Her response was, "Why didn't you send me a birthday card?" So the next year I sent her a card and called her, as well. She sounded upset, and asked, "Why don't you ever give me a birthday present?" The following year, I was determined to do it right. I picked out a special gift, then sent it along with a card. On her birthday I called and asked if she had received them. "Yeah," she said, "But I want to know why you don't come visit me on my birthday." As she keeps changing the rules for proper behavior, I just get more frustrated, and end up feeling inadequate.

Crazymakers escalate tension in normally manageable situations. In most troubled organizations, there's generally a crazymaker right at the heart of the conflict. In both families and work settings, crazymakers are usually surrounded by a circle of people who have low morale, lower quality work, and a higher absenteeism than other groups in the same setting. As self-confidence wanes, people who work around crazymakers will often ask, "Am I crazy?" or "What is wrong with me?" Supervisors, spouses, and even organizations can function as crazymakers and leave us anxious, stressed, and even sick.

Characteristics of crazymakers

Organizational consultant David Gouthro (1991) characterizes the difficult person as someone who "refuses to accept a logical rationale or argument, never listens to your point of view, appears to be intentionally obnoxious, and doesn't relate well to anything that breathes" (p. 11). In a study that looked at specific problem behaviors, University professors Craig Monroe, Mark Borzi, and Vincent DiSalvo (1989) asked 381 supervisors from nine organizations to describe characteristics of the difficult people in their organizations. The responses provided 658 critical incidents from which researchers drew conclusions. Two characteristics showed up consistently: 1) Weak self-esteem, and 2) Weak interpersonal skills.

Crazymakers share a common bond of possessing chronically low self-esteem. At some point in their lives, they developed feelings of being unappreciated, unloved, and unsupported. Because crazymakers believe that they will not be supported and respected, they manipulate and demand in order to get what they want.

Weak interpersonal skills contribute to their inappropriate communication styles. Often they don't know how to say things differently, so they just spit it out without awareness of how their messages are received.

Crazymakers usually have an inability to see others' perspectives, and as a result, don't understand why you question their decisions. Authoritarian and opinionated communication styles are common, often breeding anger and resentment in their subordinates.

Typically, crazymakers have submerged much of their feelings, leaving them with powerful work skills but an inability to feel emotions. As a result, they show little or no concern for your feelings, and have no idea why it's an issue for you. Crazymakers tend to operate as "unconscious" people, so focused on themselves that they at times don't even see you. In their presence, you can easily feel discounted, invisible and unimportant.

Characteristics of Crazymakers

- Weak self-esteem
- Weak interpersonal skills
- Inability to see other's perspective
- Inability to feel emotions or comprehend feelings
- Focused on self, "unconscious" around you

Some people become difficult at very young ages. Others developed their coping style as a result of disappointment, past failures, or personal insecurity. In spite of the negative consequences, being difficult serves as a method for accomplishing specific goals. Crazymakers are usually one of two types, *brief* or *persistent*. Anyone can become a brief or temporary crazymaker when they are tired, fearful, or stressed. Usually after a good night's sleep, or seeing improvement in the situation, the brief crazymaker returns to more functional coping styles. On the other hand, the persistent crazymaker continues to be difficult regardless of the circumstances.

What crazymakers do

Crazymakers exhibit a fairly consistent set of behaviors. Recognizing their methods will help you develop skills for managing them, instead of going crazy around them.

1. *Surprise you with requests*
   Most crazymakers are skilled in the effective use of surprise. The target person is asked to say "yes" without sufficient opportunity or time to process the request or the impact of their response. You might get an urgent call at 6 a.m., or a panicked request late Friday afternoon. Because you are caught off guard, you often agree to their demands, then later regret your decision. Often the crazymaker's lack of planning contributes to them catching you at awkward times, like the end of the work day, just before lunch, or when you are heading off to a meeting. Surprise requests will often begin with the phrase, "By the way, can you...?" and will pop up at a time when it's difficult to respond.
2. *Pressure to do something when you're unsure*
   Crazymakers are experts at manipulating and pressuring you to do something you aren't sure about. Requests are often accompanied by comments like, "It won't hurt anything, so do it just this once." Sometimes they play on fears or make subtle threats. "This might be

your only chance," or "You do want to move up in this company, don't you?"

An office worker was asked by her supervisor to back-date some documents so that he could be in compliance with company policies. When she resisted, he said, "I'm really in a jam here. Won't you please do this for me? I've done it many times in the past." She asked herself, "Why am I being pressured to solve *his* problem by doing something against company policy?" Holwitz et al., (1985) points out that the difficult person "often sends messages that demand that the other maintain a subordinate role of compliance, of relative weakness" (p. 4).

3. *Use relationships as leverage*
This persuasive tactic is common in family relationships as well as work settings. "Difficult people, when they perceive the relationship to be important to another, will use the relationship as leverage to avoid confronting more substantive issues" (Monroe et al., 1989, p. 322). Crazymakers will lean on you based on their expectation that you will do their request in order to protect the relationship. "A good daughter would go to this reunion," or "If you cared about me, you would do this favor," or "A committed employee would go the extra mile here to help the company."

4. *Isolate you from support*
Crazymakers will occasionally use manipulative behavior in groups, but generally they do their most damaging work one-on-one. When they catch you away from your support systems, you have no one to ask for advice, and must depend on your own judgment to make split-second decisions. A physician told me his 12-year-old daughter caught him as he arrived home after a long day of work. She asked if she could go to a friend's house that night for a slumber party. It was starting in an hour, so she needed a quick decision (surprise). She begged, "Please let me go. I'm old enough for you to show that you trust me. Other fathers trust their daughters (relationship for leverage). The father was very hesitant as he listened to her pleading. He didn't know the people she said were hosting the party, and it seemed rather short-notice (pressure to do something he was unsure about). He asked what her mom said, and was told mom was at work and couldn't be reached to ask her (isolation from support). Fortunately, the father made some phone calls, determined the party was a graduation celebration with no adult chaperones and a high risk of alcohol being present. Her "crazymaker tactics" failed.

5. *Shift expectations and moods*
Crazymakers are frequently unpredictable, shifting expectations just when you thought you had them figured out. Workers say, "I can

never figure out how to please my boss. Nothing I do seems to be right or good enough." Shifting expectations keeps subordinates off balance and unsure when it's okay to say something and when it's not. The ability to keep others guessing creates power that supports manipulation. "I better not say *no* because I don't want to make him mad."

Crazymakers also tend to shift frequently in their moods, going from cheerful, to angry, to apathetic, all in the same week. People around them are often confused about which way to relate to them at any given moment.

Recognizing Crazymaker Behaviors

- Surprise you with requests
- Pressure you to do something when you're unsure
- Use relationships as leverage
- Isolate you from support
- Shift expectations and moods

Crazymakers also tend to be disorganized and weak in planning skills. When they don't anticipate or plan well, they expect others to bail them out. They ask for your help and expertise to accomplish their "urgent" tasks and goals. Unfortunately, the willingness to help is rarely reciprocal. After awhile, employees become reluctant to keep sacrificing themselves when there's little affirmation or reward for their work.

In the presence of crazymakers, our self-confidence takes a beating. Because we have doubts about our ability to cope, we resort to willing compliance rather than create disappointment or anger in the crazymaker. Although giving in provides temporary escape, compliance reinforces the effectiveness of the crazymaker's tactics. The long-term impact is an unsettling anxiety in the crazymaker's presence. In many organizations morale is low, and turnover is high around the crazymaker. People who live or work in the presence of a crazymaker often get ill or depressed.

We would like crazymakers to go away, but for every one that goes away, another will come. For every difficult supervisor that leaves a company, another is hired. Frustration, anger, and escape may provide temporary relief but don't bring lasting solutions. The next section provides communication principles used by workers in industry and members of families to successfully manage crazymaker behavior. If you can't escape the crazymaker, learn to minimize their negative impact.

Crazymakers can be managed

Harvard professor Bill Ury (1991) suggests that communicating with difficult people begins with understanding what lies behind their behavior. Difficult people see the world as "eat or be eaten" and "feel justified in using nasty tactics to defend or avenge" (p. 7). They may not see the benefits of cooperative behavior and may even lack skills necessary for cooperation. They often fear losing power if they change their style. If they see the issue as win-lose, they will be resistant to discussing any options except their own. To manage crazymakers we need to use communication that does not make them more defensive than they already are, and that allows them to save face in the situation. Ury concludes, "You need to deploy your power without making an enemy who resists you even more" (p. 9).

Identify them as crazymakers

Management consultant Robert Bramson (1981) points out that identifying the difficult person "can in itself help you to take the behavior less personally. You become less paralyzed wondering what you did to bring it on and become more ready for active, more effective response" (p. 139). You know you're in the presence of a crazymaker when you're feeling pressured to do something you're not sure about (manipulation), when you don't feel your needs are understood (lack of empathy), the relationship depends on you fulfilling their request (relationship for leverage), and you feel powerless in their presence. Much of the power that crazymakers have over us can be reduced by recognizing that crazymakers don't play by the normal rules of dialogue and reciprocity in relationship. When we become aware that we are dealing with a crazymaker we employ a different set of rules.

Don't attempt to change the crazymaker

Attempting to change behaviors that have taken years or decades to develop is a frustrating and futile task. Stern words of warning, bursts of anger, and complaints about lack of understanding are often met with a deaf ear by the crazymaker. They may in fact increase their level of obnoxious behaviors. Bramson (1981) suggests that the most valuable single step is to "stop wishing they were different...The attempt to change or blame is an exercise in futility that only sidetracks you from what you *can* do to alleviate the situation" (p. 136-137).

It is useless to get into a battle of control with the crazymaker. Generally, they are skilled at manipulating, producing guilt feelings, and getting their own way. Don't attempt to change or control the crazymaker. Instead focus on communication that minimizes the crazymakers control over you.

Don't expect them to respond to feelings

When we experience conflict with a difficult person, we sometimes resort to appealing to their emotional side. We say things like, "Don't you care how I feel?" Unfortunately, they usually don't, or at least consider your feelings to be unrelated to their current needs or demands.

Recognize that a crazymaker won't be likely to respond on an emotional level. Using more factual statements as opposed to "feeling" words will probably improve your communication outcomes.

Don't let them spoil your day

Sometimes it will seem like the crazymaker has an agenda to "get you." We need to emotionally separate our identity and self-esteem from their negative behaviors. By not giving them power in our life, we maintain a stronger sense of integrity and confidence about out work. Maintain a sense of humor, depersonalize what they're saying, and get some distance from them when you can.

When you deal with crazymakers on a regular basis, you need to work on managing them on two different levels. The first level is managing yourself in their presence, learning how to minimize the impact they have on you. The second level involves responding to their demands in ways that enhance your communication and ability to relate. Intentionally using specific skills in your interactions can change their ability to drive you crazy or hurt your work relationship. With practice, you can learn how to relate to a difficult colleague or family members in ways that bring surprising results and often alter the relationship outcomes.

Manage *yourself* in a crazymaker's presence

You can decrease a crazymaker's power by carefully managing your responses to their behaviors. Sometimes this involves using caution with your words or actions, while other times it means leaving for a few minutes to collect your thoughts.

- *Monitor your physical and nonverbal responses*
  Crazymakers have confided that they feel empowered when they see others irritated, frustrated, or anxious. An emotional response heightens the possibility that they'll get what they want, especially if they

turn up the pressure another notch. Crazymakers know they have greater power in the situation if they perceive the target person is feeling helpless or worrying about how to meet expectations. If we are in a reactive mode, the chances are greater that we'll say something we'll regret. Remaining emotionally neutral to the crazymaker's behavior will help you be more effective in determining the best strategy for communicating your preferences and needs. By minimizing the emotional component, which is where the crazymaker finds power, you can focus on substantive issues that utilize your knowledge and skills.

Monitoring your nonverbal responses, like rolling your eyes, grimacing, or pounding your fist, will decrease their awareness of whether their manipulation tactics are working. This doesn't mean you should never show your feelings. But you can practice the skill of postponing expressions of emotion until you are away from their presence. Tell yourself you will allow yourself to feel it and show how you feel, as soon as you get to a private setting. This works well for tears, as well as anger, frustration, and disgust.

Sometimes it helps to protect yourself from the situation for awhile. Getting some distance from a crazymaker gives you a chance to regain your perspective and return to a more logical understanding of the issue. Distancing also helps if you need to regain your composure or calm your anger and frustration. Regain the balance between your logic and your emotions. Try to avoid soaking up their tension or being stressed because they are uptight. Protecting yourself will keep you from getting caught up in their style and becoming a crazymaker yourself. One employee told me she joked more with her boss. When she came back from lunch and he growled, "Where have you been?" She responded with a perky, "Hi, did you miss me?"

• *Reduce isolation*
Crazymakers love to isolate their target from sources of emotional support or information that might reveal problems in their expectations or requests. Two weeks before Christmas Mike was asked to do a two-hour program for a state agency. The person making the request pushed his guilt buttons with her appeal, "We need what you have to offer. You'll help me out a lot by agreeing to do the program. The staff depends on me finding someone to speak that day." Mike expressed his feelings and reservations concerning the timing, but she continued her appeal. He questioned the necessity of the program being so close to Christmas, and expressed concerns about the receptivity of the staff to training, the location for the program, and his ability to meet the expectations of the group. He felt pressured to do something he didn't want to do.

When he asked about payment for doing the program, she said, "There is no payment for this program but if the staff likes it, they will probably want to schedule further training with payment later in the year." Mike was still uncomfortable, so he delayed his response.

Later that day he spoke with a colleague who was a specialist in the group's subject area. He told Mike that he did an eight-hour program for the group last year. They were not very receptive to the program, he was not paid, nor did the group schedule further training. By reducing isolation, Mike uncovered information that helped him deal more confidently and effectively with the person who requested the program. When we are unsure about an issue, postponing actions or decisions can decrease the risk of saying yes under pressure. Tell the crazymaker you need to think about it, then reduce your isolation. Expressing your doubts and concerns to another person will help you clarify your thinking and be more effective in decision making.

- *Manage and communicate expectations*
What we expect from others and how we communicate those expectations becomes more important when dealing with crazymakers. If we have a rigid or fixed picture of how organizations should operate, we will be frustrated by behaviors of people who have different goals and different agendas. The more we expect crazymakers to think or act the way we do, the more difficult it will be to relate to them. Behavioral scientists Michael Lombardo and Morgan McCall (1989) at the Center for Creative Leadership in Greensboro, North Carolina propose that, "Most of us begin our work life incredibly naive about organizations. We expect our particular vision of rationality to prevail, and when it doesn't, we become cynical" (p. 46). One way to prevail around crazymakers is to develop a realistic view of what can be accomplished in that setting.

Lack of success in managing expectations is reflected in the research of University of Pennsylvania psychology professor Martin Seligman (1988) who found that Americans today are *ten* times more likely to get depressed than their grandparents.

We come to expect our jobs to be more than a way to make a living. Work now needs to be ecological innocent, comforting to our dignity, a call to growth and excitement, a meaningful contribution to society and deliver a large paycheck. Married partners once settled for duty but today's mates expect to be ecstatic lovers, intellectual colleagues, and partners at tennis and water sports. (p. 52)

Soaring expectations of how family members and colleagues *should* behave gets in the way of effective communication. Sometimes people's behavior is difficult for us because our expectations are unrealistic. We need to focus on what's possible, recognizing that some goals are impossible to attain.

In addition to realistic expectations about what the crazymaker is willing to do or is capable of doing, it helps to create clear and specific expectations. For example,

I'm sorry I didn't get the details of the report the way you wanted them (shifting expectations). It will help me if you could write down some specific things you'd like done, so I can match how you want it.

I'd really like to help you out but I need more advance notice. Perhaps you could let me work on my schedule and I'll clear a block of time for you.

I really value doing a good job. Here's a few things I need to help me work better. Also, here are some obstacles that get in my way. Maybe you can help me a little with each of these.

When communicating expectations, plan to discuss them at a time when you can do it without emotion and then make them as specific as possible. Crazymakers rarely respond to generalities such as, "I need respect" or "I need your support." They do better with specifics such as, "I need these reports by this date and in this manner," or "When you make these requests on Friday afternoon, I don't have sufficient time to work on them. I need more time if you want them approved." Some crazymakers do not process needs and expectations very well verbally. By communicating with them in a written form, they may understand your request better.

Techniques for managing crazymakers

Awareness of yourself and how you respond around crazymakers will improve your effectiveness with managing them. The next set of skills involves specific techniques to use in their presence. When you can't avoid crazymakers or make them go away, these skills will often lead to more positive outcomes in your interactions.

- *Slow the crazymaker down*
  To reduce the power of surprise and to regain personal control, use communication that slows the crazymaker down. Give yourself time to process requests and sufficiently weigh alternatives. Responding with, "Let me get back to you," buys you time to think and avoid a pressured decision. Crazymakers use tactics familiar to sales people, "You'd better act now or you'll lose this opportunity." Decisions are often made quickly and without full consideration of the implications. "Disconnect the automatic link between emotion and action. Suspend your impulses; freeze your behavior. Be quick to hear, slow to speak, slow to act" (Ury, 1989, p. 29). An important technique is to speak slowly, using a *low* tone of voice. Avoid escalating or raising your voice in response to theirs. When they talk faster and louder, simply drop back to speaking slower and quieter. Many confrontations can be avoided by consciously monitoring your voice and not escalating your pace to match their angry or frenzied words.

- *Ask lots of questions*
  Asking questions will help you divide big issues into smaller, more manageable pieces. Consider the image of eating a whole salami at once. For most people, this would be overwhelming, perhaps resulting in a stomach ache or feeling sick. A more manageable approach would be to cut and eat a slice at a time. Many employees or family members deal with crazymakers and stressful situations by taking on the entire problem at once. Taking a "salami approach" by breaking it down into slices of manageable tasks, will often give better results.

  Asking lots of questions and clarifying issues helps you sort crazymakers demands and determine what they really want. John, was asked by his supervisor to come in on Saturday to help finish a report. John's immediate reaction was anger and resentment. He had lots of plans for the weekend, and wanted to spend time with his family. He considered protesting and saying he couldn't do it, but decided to ask questions instead:

  > *When is the report due?*
  > *What still needs to be done?*
  > *How much Saturday time will be necessary?*
  > *Could we shift some work on Monday and finish it then?*
  > *Which part of the report do you need help with?*

As they sat in John's office, calmly discussing the questions, the supervisor began considering other options, and ultimately decided that the report could wait. Crazymakers will often look for a quick solution to reduce their stress without considering the implications of what they ask. Questions help us explore and evaluate options, as well as helping us maintain control over our reactions.

Crazymakers often resist looking at alternatives. Sometimes we can break an impasse by using the communications technique, *broken record*. This involves repeating the same phrase or idea with slight changes in the wording. Broken record works best if you acknowledge or affirm the other person first, then state what you want.

> *Yes, that report is really important, but I'd like to work on it Friday or Monday instead of the weekend.*
>
> *You really have been swamped this week, but I'd like to come in early on Monday to do the report.*
>
> *Yes, the boss has been pressuring us lately, but I'd like to work on the report early on Monday.*

Even though this technique won't always work, it seems to encourage the other person to consider alternatives and rethink their initial decision.

- *Communicate understanding*
  Demands at times exceed the coping abilities of many people. Stresses from home or work can turn people who normally communicate easily into brief or temporary crazymakers. This becomes a time to decrease demands and instead verbalize understanding and concern. Bramson (1981) reminds us that "understanding can provide the necessary vantage point that will release you from those patterns of interaction that bring out the worst in everyone" (p. 140). For example, airline pilots work with crews who must spend prolonged periods of time away from home. The nature of the work at times creates brief crazymakers, but the airplane staff must deal with conflict for the sake of both the crew and the passengers. Delta Airlines pilot John Mayer says it's a challenge when your co-pilot is a crazymaker, but you must work it through. His remedy begins with understanding:

> *Talk to them on a personal level. Try to figure out where they're coming from. People don't want to be jerks just to be jerks. you could talk to them about something you have in common, such as family. I ask, 'Is there anything I can do for you?' They're stressed out. They're fearful. They may feel overloaded.*

When you communicate understanding and help them with their stress, you can become their friend rather than the one they make crazy.

In many organizations, there are reasons why some individuals have developed crazymaking behaviors. When relationships deteriorated between an administration department and their major client firms, the clients identified the department supervisor as a crazymaker. They complained that he set objectives and standards that caused problems, then pressured them to achieve them anyway. When the supervisor resigned, the situation didn't change. Further exploration revealed that the supervisor's boss, a vice president, was forcing him to insist on the goals and standards. At times we need to be slower to judge a crazymaker until we know more about the dynamics that support their behavior.

- *Minimize rigid thinking*
Sometimes managing a crazymaker becomes easier when we decrease our own level of rigid thinking. We tend to get stuck on how they *should* act, and give ourselves stress because they don't match our picture. Changing rigid thinking begins with a willingness to consider options beyond our own view. Allowing the possibility that an issue could be approached differently and still work will often eliminate the battle.

A friend tells about typical conversations she would hear from her parents. Dad would say, "Your uncle stopped by to see us last Tuesday." Mom would interrupt with, "It wasn't Tuesday because that's the day it rained...." My friend's frustration was, "Who cares what day they came! I was happy to know they had dropped by for a visit."

We hold a mental picture of our expectations for many things in life. The smaller or more rigid the picture, the more likely we will experience conflict or stress. When our expectations are extremely rigid, life will almost never match our view of how it *should be*. At times we need to consciously explore the question, "Could it be some other way, and still work?" By altering our rigid view of the "right" way to do things, we can decrease a lot of our conflict. Affirming a crazymaker by saying, "It possibly could work that way," will often open a more productive dialogue.

- *Go "deaf" to destructive comments*
When crazymakers don't get their way, they frequently make statements designed to cause emotional pain such as, "You've never been there for me," or "You sure aren't the worker (friend) that I thought you were." The comments are designed to manipulate or to create a heightened state of guilt and anxiety. It's useful to go "emotionally deaf" to the harmful comments and instead focus discussion on interests

and need. Business consultant Roberta Cava (1990) suggests, "Mentally throw a negative comment in the garbage can. Don't pass it on, even when everyone else seems to. When people take out their bad feelings on you, remember that you can choose not to accept them" (p. 58).

One way to manage destructive messages is to *redirect attention* from personal attacks to less emotional content of the messages. For example:

Crazymaker:	If you had checked with me, you would have found out that we do things different around here.
Intended victim:	Maybe you can help me here. Which procedures do you think I should run by you before taking action?
Crazymaker:	If you cared about your job, you'd stay late and help me.
Intended victim:	I care about my job and I care about helping you. But tell me more. What do you need and how can my staying late make a difference?

Both examples attempt to move the crazymaker from an attacking perspective and into specific issues. In order to redirect attacks, we must be open to feedback and to exploring underlying issues that make crazymakers behave the way they do. Ury (1991) recommends a variety of methods for reframing destructive comments:

> *Reframe an attack on you as an attack on the problem. Perceive a personal attack as friendly or as a show of concern. Focus on future remedies rather than past mistakes. Instead of using "me" and "you," speak in terms of "we," suggesting a "We're in this together" approach. (p. 73-76)*

For example:

| *Crazymaker:* | Aren't you smart enough to know that you're just wasting our time at staff meetings by bringing up new projects with little or no chance of approval? |
| *Intended victim:* | You make a good point. What needs to be done in order to make my proposals more appealing so that they might get full consideration at our meetings? |

Crazymaker:	No one in this department has any sense about how to get things done.
Intended victim:	It sounds as though you've got some ideas about more effective procedures. Tell me about them.

In each of the examples, the intended victim avoids becoming defensive and reframes the messages from personal attacks to attacks on the issue.

Are they really crazymakers?

A person may be a crazymaker for you and may not be for someone else. When you see a crazymaker relating well to a colleague or supervisor it doesn't mean that you will have similar luck. Sometimes crazymakers have favorite employees they seem to relate with quite easily. Perhaps your past history shapes your perceptions of the crazymaker. They may remind you of someone in your past that you didn't like or with whom you didn't get along. Sometimes the organizational dynamics create hidden agendas and pressures that influence interpersonal interactions. Whatever the reason, the quality of the relationship and the level of stress depends on our ability to devise an effective strategy for communicating with the crazymaker.

Begin with a self-awareness that you're around someone who says and does things differently than you expect. Identify the behaviors that trigger negative reactions, then slow down the pace of interactions so you can create an effective response. Shift the focus away from a battle of control and toward resolution of specific issues. At times the crazymaker wants to give you his or her problem. Evaluate whether it is worth *your stress* to solve *their problem*. Manage your personal response to guilt appeals, and reduce isolation by getting support from trusted friends and colleagues. By reducing the counter-productive cycles that escalate tension, we can create a pattern where our communication effectively manages the crazymaker's behavior.

CHAPTER NINE

Difficult Organizational Settings

"Toto, something tells me we're not in Kansas anymore."
Dorothy in *Wizard of Oz*
by L. Frank Baum

In the *Wizard of Oz*, Dorothy was suddenly tossed high into the air by a swirling tornado. After she landed in Oz, she spend the rest of the story asking, "Where am I, how did I get here, and how can I get back home?"

In many organizations, workers ask the same questions. Difficult work settings can even cause workers who normally do well to question their skills and effectiveness. Some difficult organizations have always been that way, a result of poor leadership or weak corporate vision. Occasionally they are headed by crazymakers whose disorganization and lack of people skills set the tone for the entire operation.

But in many cases, companies that originally existed as enjoyable, productive settings undergo a change, as though swept by the winds of Dorothy's tornado. Rapid growth without corresponding changes in personnel, systems, and planning can transform a work group from friends to near enemies. As technology advances, the workpace often speeds to a frenzied level, simultaneously weakening interpersonal links and creating more conflict.

The drive for corporate profits often translates into employees being pressured to work harder or produce more. When workers describe high levels of stress in their work setting, there's often someone at the top who is determined to impact the bottom line and increase profits. Top-level managers can become equally caught in this corporate vision, and pressure their departments and employees to match their intensity.

Downsizing and reengineering create another set of issues for workers. Fear of lay-offs, as well as unknowns with respect to buyouts or changes in

139

leadership, contribute to added stress within employee ranks. Some companies become hyperturbulent environments, settings characterized by a fast changing pace with instability of structure, ideas, and personnel. As the work setting becomes more difficult, employees struggle with declining morale, decreasing trust levels and weakening belief in the organization as a whole.

Difficult settings, like difficult people, possess characteristics that are a challenge to overcome. Factors common to many difficult organizational settings include:

- Procedures and systems in a state of change
- Job responsibilities that fluctuate and often lack clarity
- Unclear organizational goals
- Inadequate processes for conflict management
- Interpersonal relationships lack trust; communication often secretive

Although the above factors are fairly universal in difficult settings, specific corporate changes will often create additional communication challenges.

Reengineering settings

Restructuring of procedures, personnel and decision-making processes or personnel creates challenges for communication in organizations. Unclear procedures and loss of continuity with the past often accompany multiple changes. For example, contractors who work with AT&T complain that the corporation's reduction of middle management, who served as predictable points of contact, make it difficult to locate resources for handling problems. Workers within AT&T describe poor coordination between divisions, and duplication of efforts. After reengineering began at US West Communications, one worker said, "Some divisions don't know what others are doing, and at times we send customers conflicting messages." Changes in leadership and procedures create ambiguity and occasionally leave workers wondering, "Who's in charge?" In reengineering environments many workers lose a sense of organizational direction, vision, and corporate goals. New Technologies specialists Robert Johansen and Rob Swigart (1996) conclude,

Reengineering and restructuring have left many of today's corporations, especially the large ones, filled with gaps in their structure and lapses in their continuity. Some large corporations are now so filled with holes that they have little sense of themselves as complete entities. (p. 86-87)

Reengineering isn't going away. Statistics show that great numbers of organizations are going through downsizing and restructuring.

Reengineering by Industry (n = 982)

All Industries	Manufacturing	Transportation/ Communication	Business Services	Health Services	Public Administration
35%	47%	48%	24%	36%	47%

(Source: "1995 Industry Report")

Downsizing environments

One type of reenginnering that has received a lot of attention in the past decade is termed downsizing by some organizations, rightsizing by others. In spite of lay-offs that have already occurred, industry analysts estimated that another 25% of the workforce is still subject to downsizing (Sherman, 1991).

Downsizing by Industry (n = 982)

All Industries	Manufacturing	Transportation/ Communication	Business Services	Health Services	Public Administration
31%	28%	42%	31%	46%	47%

(Source: "1995 Industry Report")

A 1990 survey conducted by Right Associates, an outplacement firm, identified ways downsizing impacts employees. In the survey, 75% of senior managers in downsized organizations reported low morale of workers, problems linked to trust, and a decline of productivity (Henkoff, 1990). In a recent survey by the American Management Association of organizations that downsized between 1989-1994, decreased morale emerged as a central factor:

Outcomes of Downsizing

	Increased	Remained Constant	Declined
Operating Profits	50.6%	29.1%	20.4%
Worker Productivity	34.4%	35.5%	30.1%
Employee Morale	1.9%	12.1%	86%

(Source: "Some Companies Cut")

Not only is the number of workers changing, but also the nature of the workforce. Companies are using greater numbers of temporary or industry-mobile workers who have less emotional investment in the organization and minimal commitment to long-term needs.

Use of Industry-mobile Workers by Industry (n= 982)

All Industries	Manufacturing	Transportation/ Communication	Business Services	Health Services	Public Administration
21%	23%	17%	25%	19%	27%

(Source: "1995 Industry Report")

The current trend in hiring workers who will be with an organization for only a few years will not decline soon. Castro (1993) estimates that by the year 2000, the ratio of temporary workers to permanent employees in the American workforce will be almost equal. Organizations who use a high number of temporary workers often experience undesirable changes:

• Lower level of commitment to organizational goals
• Lack of unity on staffs
• Weaker loyalty to the organization
• Lack of incentive to develop long-term relationships

Environmental hyperturbulence

In one of Woody Allen's comedy routines, he describes his experience playing the cello in his high school marching band. Because he was small and the cello so large, he'd have to sit down to be able to play. Every time the band would stop, he'd put his chair down and play a few notes. But he'd only be seated a few moments before the band would march past him so he would have to stand up, move his chair and his cello forward, play a few notes, stand up, and again move forward. He was never able to keep up. Many people feel this way about the organizations in which they work. Just about the time they get effective procedures in place, there are changes in personnel, policies, and even department goals. The environment keeps passing them by.

Environmental turbulence describes organizational settings in which "environmental demands finally exceed the collective adaptive capacities of members sharing an environment" (McCann & Selsky, 1984, p. 460). Current hyperturbulent corporate environments are characterized by intense competitiveness, fast pace of technological advancements, and many frequent changes. Few organizations are exempt from at least occasional periods of hyperturbelence. For example, the health care industry has gone through massive reorganization in just the past few years. Telecommunications are growing faster than resources and structures comfortably support. Advances in computer technology occur continuously. The adaptive capacity of present communication processes are stretched to their limits.

One of the factors that contributes to hyperturbulent environments is the information explosion. The quantity of information available doubled each year between 1990 and 1995. Estimates are that by 2025 information will double each month. At a communications firm, workers from the marketing division complained that the research and development division wasn't keeping up with advances made by competitors. On the other hand representatives from sales expressed concern that development of new products was faster than their ability to understand how the products worked. One group believes that development is too slow and the other group thinks it's too fast. This corporation's growth pattern was challenging communication among all departments.

Not only is there a high volume of information in hyperturbulent settings, the information is occasionally unclear, ambiguous, or complex. Workers ask questions such as, "How does the new information fit with what we're already planning?" or "Who needs the information and when do they need it?" A program developer complained that it was difficult for him to plan when he couldn't get a clear breakdown of information from marketing. "The numbers you give me could imply many things." Marketing staff responded, "We don't have systems in place to give you the kind of breakdown you need." Tension occurs when there's a high volume of information and limited understanding of what the information means.

Daft et al. (1993) point out that "organizational environments that are unpredictable and changing often provide managers a messy, unclear field of view. People or groups can reach very different, yet equally definable conclusions after observing the same objective clues" (p. 113).

Advances in communication technology

The growth of electronic forms of communication have reshaped the business environment. Compared to costs of travel and time in meetings, many consider e-mail, voice mail, and faxes, to be faster, cheaper, and to provide greater distribution. The number of people who subscribe and draw information from the Internet is sky-rocketing. Johansen and Swigart (1996) suggest that, "electronic media are seeping into the cracks in the traditional business infrastructure which introduces basic questions about how work itself is organized" (p. 161-162).

Electronic-based communication sometimes creates problems that impact interpersonal relationships. For example, in some organizations lack of privacy has contributed to decreased levels of trust. Computer monitoring has become common, at times even the subject of lawsuits. Because electronic communication filters out many of the nonverbal cues of interpersonal communication, there is less confidence about how receivers react to or understand messages. Sproull and Kiesler (1986) found in their study of electronic communication in manufacturing firms, that workers felt less inhibited about communicating frankly, and sent a greater number of messages perceived as hostile. An employee from a computer firm lamented, "My supervisor sends me e-mail that contains angry messages followed by frowning faces." In addition, Sproull and Kiesler also found that 40% of those who used electronic mail did not know the gender of receivers and 32% lacked knowledge about the status of receivers. These unknowns heighten the potential for misunderstanding or conflict. Organizational communication scholars Patricia Andrews and Richard Herschel (1996) conclude, "The new technologies do not necessarily replace interpersonal communication through more traditional media but rather exist alongside them, as other options which individuals may choose" (p. 119).

Communication in the Land of Oz

Joe Staszik served for 23 years as director of the Latin American Book Program for the US Information Agency in Mexico City. This organization produces books in 12 languages that are used overseas for US public relations. They also facilitate cultural and educational programs, and for 25 years produced the *Voice of America* program for broadcast in the Soviet Union. Staszik worked with representatives of foreign governments, the US State Government, and the US Government Services Agency. Based on a long history of working with difficult organizations, Staszik offers the following suggestions for people who work in difficult organizations:

- Understand how the organization works. Each group has rules, regulations and policies. Trace decision-making processes back to their source and attempt to understand how they operate.
- Personalize the process. Stereotyping the whole organization as "difficult" creates perceptual barriers. There are people in every organization who care about the work and getting things done effectively. Identify the caring people and establish a working relationship. They can become your contacts for working around problem points in the organization.
- Pursue people with competence within the system. Find someone who knows what they're talking about.

Staszik tells about how he once tried to reach a colleague at a corporation by calling extension 3277. Someone answered, "How can I help you?" Staszik said, "I would like to talk to Mr. Johnson." The operator responded, "Mr. Johnson is at extension 3297." So Staszik hung up and called 3297. The same person answered the phone. When Staszik said, "Didn't I just talk to you?" the operator responded, "Yes I answer the phone for both extensions." This person will probably not be a lot of help in getting things done. Staszik suggests that we recognize this early, and as we are able, avoid the people who frustrate the process or are "obvious know-nothings." Staszik believes in connecting with those around you:

Show an interest in what people are doing. Establish a bond with them. They will be more willing to help you with your problems if they believe you're interested in theirs. As there is opportunity, make an offer to help those whose cooperation will be useful to you later. Watch for opportunities to befriend those who help make the system work.

Staszik tells about an experience as he waited in an airport in the Philippines on his way to Milan, Italy. He befriended two men who were relaxing in the airport lounge. One of the men had misplaced his wallet, so Staszik bought a drink for both of them. Later that evening, when Staszik found that his luggage was mistakenly on a plane that was headed for New Delhi, he sought help from airport personnel. As the plane was backing out of the gate, airport security ran out, stopped the plane and retrieved Staszik's luggage. The man who interceded on his behalf was the director of airport security, one of the two men he previously befriended in the airport lounge. The other man, he found out later, was president of the World Bank, and a prominent financial figure. Staszik recommends:

Don't give up easily in your attempts to work with difficult systems. Be like a computer hacker who keeps trying until he gets into the computer system. Be flexible enough to work with their system and respect their hierarchy. If you satisfy their needs they're less likely to get in your way.

Keep messages appropriate

One way to reduce some of the problems in difficult work environments is to focus on using the appropriate message for the situation. Some forms of communication provide better delivery of information or symbolic value than others. Long detailed instructions lend themselves better to written communication than to e-mail messages. Feedback concerning job performance requires face-to-face discussion rather than a memo. Consider the symbolic impact carried by the form of the message. A company supervisor used an e-mail message to congratulate an employee for 20 years of work. The impersonal nature of this form of communication, symbolically communicated insincerity and a lack of appreciation. Another employee complained that her supervisor would use memos to inform her of changes. She interpreted this to mean that the supervisor was avoiding her, and lacked sufficient trust in her to deliver the message face-to-face. Supervisors at an oil firm were prohibited from talking with employees about job openings in their departments. Information could be shared only by posting the job on the cafeteria bulletin board. Workers concluded that the leaders preferred decision-making procedures that were secretive and conducted in closed-door meetings.

A bank officer was frustrated with an elderly client who kept having problems with his loan account. He kept writing his loan payments using outdated checks and sending them to the wrong address. Numerous telephone calls didn't seem to correct the situation. Finally the bank requested that he come in person to discuss the problem. As the bank officer began talking with the client, she realized that he was very hard of hearing. Speaking slowly and clearly with the checkbook in front of him, she was able to help him understand the problem. He expressed his appreciation and admitted to her that he could hear very little over the phone. Recognizing the needs and styles of employees will help improve communication effectiveness. Some people don't like talking on the phone, and simply prefer face-to-face or a written message. Others try to manage their time by using e-mail as opposed to phone calls to communicate brief messages. Communication will be enhanced by careful choice of an appropriate form, as well as respecting the needs of the receiver.

In many difficult settings, using multiple channels helps reduce misunderstanding for the sharing of information. In a study of 50 manufacturers, Daft et al. (1988) found that the highest performing firms in hyperturbulent settings relied on multiple channels for both obtaining and sharing information. Information on corporate decisions might first be discussed face-to-face in order to create shared understandings. Telephone conversations and e-mail messages can provide additions or corrections. Eventually, a memo which summarizes the conclusions may help clarify the new corporate directives.

Based on a study of 59 Texas firms, Daft et al. (1993) provide insight into selecting the appropriate form of communication. They concluded that face-to-face communication is best for creating new organizational procedures, while technology-based forms work better within established frameworks. Organizational procedures require authority, legitimacy, and symbolic implications, so the potential for compliance is heightened by participation in the discussions. On the other hand, once a framework and procedures are established, technology-based communication forms work well. Letters, e-mail, memos, and phone mail clarify technical information and procedures.

During the Gulf war, it would have been faster for President Bush to make decisions based on information he received by way of telephone conversations and other electronic media. Yet when it came to vital decisions, he sent Secretary of State Robert Cheney and Joint Chief of Staff Colin Powell to Kuwait for first-hand observation of the situation and face-to-face conversations with Gulf Commander Norman Schwarzkoph. Research supports Bush's strategy around major decisions. Supervisors have found that oral messages followed by written ones are highly effective when needs require immediate action, policy changes, or major company decisions (Level, 1972).

Negotiate common understandings

In difficult settings we tend to adopt tougher stances. We might say things like, "Here's where I draw the line," or "I can't be pushed any further." These responses escalate conflict and build walls that are counterproductive to good relationships or productive processes. Communication behaviors that negotiate common understanding will promote greater willingness to cooperate.

Negotiating how information fits, as well as its significance or its priority, becomes an essential skill in settings where information is changing rapidly. Because contexts are more complex than a decade ago, both management and staff must engage in give-and-take discussions to shape common understandings that might guide tasks.

Ways to Negotiate Common Understanding

- Avoid using threats
- Make small concessions in order to demonstrate commitment
- Emphasize solutions where all parties will achieve gain
- Express a willingness to admit error if it removes barriers in the relationship
- Allow others to save face by utilizing the best interpretation of behaviors

---

Occasionally, problems with negotiating or engaging in cooperative discussions results from our inability to listen without passing immediate judgments. Roethlisberger (1988) suggests that the "major barrier to mutual interpersonal understanding is the natural tendency to judge, evaluate, to approve (or disapprove) the statement of the other" (p. 193). For example, when a colleague says, "This new project looks like it has major problems," you can respond by saying, "I agree. We're being asked to do something that doesn't make sense." Or you can say, "I'm not sure I agree. I think the plan looks fine." With either response, we evaluate the issue from *our* frame of reference.

Judgmental evaluation prohibits shared understandings or constructive problem solving. To overcome this barrier, we must resist the desire to evaluate and judge and focus our energy on deeper understanding the issue. In the above example, an alternate response might be, "What is it about the project that's causing you concern?" Instead of rehearsing whether issues are good or bad we should work on understanding the whys and the meanings of the problems.

Balance the need for control

In difficult settings we also need to balance the need for control. When we get frustrated, we often exert control by trying to fix people or organizational dynamics that rarely respond to our efforts. Remember the gentleman who was trying to change Medicare? Battling forces over which we have little influence does not make good use of our energies.

Because of the complexity of people and situations, control is often an illusion. It's like having two roller skates linked together with a foot-long spring. As the two skates roll together, one controls the other in a tenuous manner. Now attach a third and a fourth skate with the same kind of springs. Though all are attached with the same lines, control becomes more difficult without cooperation. Organizations are infinitely more complex then a simple line of roller skates and springs. You can see why a person dictating orders from "one end of the line" cannot possibly control what happens in a complex organization (Senge, 1990, p. 290).

Psychologist Susan Campbell (1995) suggests, "If we are to move gracefully in a world of nonstop change and global interdependence, we must develop an entirely new direction of what it means to be in control" (p. 27). We must balance our need for control with an awareness that others have that same need. We must become aware of the limits of our influence and resist trying to mold organizations and people into the way we'd like them to be. There is a time to push for change, but there is also a time to adapt to realities. Nibble at the edges for small changes and work to accomplish change in areas where change is possible.

Control in Organizational Settings

Instead of	Try
Attempting to force others to do things your way	Allowing others to do things in different ways
Getting frustrated by ineffective organizational procedures	Looking for small changes that enable you to live with the procedures
Fixating on what should be	Seeing things the way they are
Thinking in terms of either/or	Thinking in terms of both/and
Trying to coerce to your side	Attempt to influence to your point of view

---

Manage ambiguity

Ambiguous or unclear messages frequently cause frustration in organizational communication. Prior to her business trip to Asia, a manager called a department meeting. She announced that profit shortfalls would require a major tightening of budgets. In addition, she asked the staff to warmly welcome the three new employees who were joining the organization. Her ambiguous message seemed to be, "We are short of money," yet she was traveling extensively and hiring new employees. By clarifying the reasoning behind the decisions, she would decrease her staff's frustration and confusion as to whether the company was short of money.

In difficult work settings, where there is rapid change and a high volume of ambiguous information, there is a greater need for face-to-face discussions where issues are explained. By enhancing common understanding, there is shared ownership of processes and goals. Daft et al. (1993) explain,

> *An example of this approach is the communication required to bring about a new business strategy. Since multiple interpretations of the competitive environment are available, debate and feedback among managers enable them to agree about the meaning of information so that a strategic direction can be established (p. 117).*

At the same time there must be caution about group discussion in difficult settings. There is a tendency for groups to deteriorate into gripe sessions, tangential discussions, and rehearsals of old conflicts. Effective leaders keep the members focused on specific issues and away from the need to assess blame. They must try to resolve ambiguities with regard to responsibility, specific policies, or goals, and avoid getting trapped in philosophical discussions of ideals and what should be. In difficult settings philosophical discussion can accentuate conflict and further polarize staff. Employees need explanation at all levels about what we do and why we do it. "When individuals do not understand the reasons behind change, they may view it as an unnecessary annoyance, dreamed up by managers just to complicate their lives, and may see only the drawbacks associated with the change" (Paulis et al. 1996, p. 473).

Communication professors Dominic Infante and William Gorden (1985) found that people report the highest levels of satisfaction in organizational environments where they can engage in constructive argument, confront differences of opinion, and offer candid feedback in efforts to reach common understandings. Creating this kind of environment requires members who are open to information and opinions that differ from their own and have the skill to negotiate the meaning of the information. Harvard negotiation professors Fisher, Kopelman and Schneider (1994) suggest, "Doing better is not a matter of producing good answers out of thin air, but a matter of asking a series of questions which are likely to result in coping more skillfully with an endless flow of conflict interests" (p. 144).

Structural inertia

In contrast to the fast changing, unpredictable factors associated with hyperturbulent or reengineering environments, some organizations become trapped in a tortoise-like pace of settings constrained by procedural or structural inertia. Change occurs slowly. Strong social or political norms inhibit doing things differently even if the changes are positive. In difficult organizations, this pattern becomes extremely frustrating for workers who value efficiency or effective processes. In organizations slowed by inertia, workers often say, "Why bother to try? It won't make a difference anyway."

An organization immobilized by structural inertia may be characterized by members who are apathetic, who do not collaborate effectively as a team, and who appear resigned to the way things are. People within the organization resign themselves to organizational procedures they dislike, but don't know how to change. You must be strategic in these settings to get what you need. Knowing who to call, how to talk to them, and what to ask for become important issues for overcoming inertia-bound organizational procedures.

Milt Robinson, who worked for 33 years with the US Forest Service, describes the difficulty his department encountered when trying to obtain information from the Department of Interior. Because they made decisions about land and resource management, the Forest Service would often receive requests for information on the amount of minerals, such as coal, oil, and gas, that were being mined from certain areas of land. Since the Department of the Interior managed the data on the mineral levels, Forest Service personnel would contact them to request the most current information.

The Department of the Interior seemed to be stuck in structural inertia, with very antiquated computer systems and inefficient procedures for gathering information. Sometimes it would take up to six months to obtain data, and then it often would be inaccurate or incomplete. The Forest Service had no leverage or incentive for encouraging the Department of Interior to address their needs.

Robinson decided that the way to overcome the interia was to change the way the Forest Service communicated with the Interior Department. They began by obtaining organizational charts from the Department of Interior. They identified personnel who would know the data they needed. They made phone calls to verify the accuracy of the responsibilities outlined by the chart. Then they arranged meetings with these employees and asked questions like, "How can we help you get the answers?" and "Can we help program your computer software to speed access to the data we need?"

In addition, the Forest Service budgeted money that could be used to pay for staff in the Interior Department when they spent extra time on the computer getting the data. They set up quarterly meetings to improve dialogue between the two agencies. Robinson says, "We needed them to see us as fellow government employees responding to needs of citizens and not as members of a rival agency." The Forest Service provided unexpected benefits to the Interior Department by uncovering glitches in their data base and helping them correct the problems. Robinson summarizes his principles for working with organizations that are entrenched in structural inertia:

1. Respect the chain of command of organizations and the status of their workers.
2. Get to know their staff in a non-threatening way. Build relationships before the need arises to discuss difficult issues such as budget, laws and regulations, and policy changes. The relationship that you build will make it easier to get work done.
3. Ask them open-ended questions and listen carefully to responses. Don't offer advise unless asked to. Keep your mouth shut and observe. Get to know who the players are and what they feel is important.
4. Understand what makes their procedures difficult. Try to determine the specific points that you have problems with. Think it through, have responses ready for problems you anticipate.
5. Become part of the solution, not another problem for them. In the above example, the Forest Service specifically asked, "How can we help you provide the data we need?"

Robinson recommends, "Don't say, 'Do it because I said to do it.' Communicate that you understand their problems and concerns and that you realize how requests for change will affect them."

Handling Difficult Situations

DCI Corporation

DCI provides communication products and services for a metropolitan city. B. Shot is director of a department that has eight units, each with six to eight members and a manager.

Darla and Buelah work in two of these DCI units. Buelah is manager of a unit charged with managing upkeep on all computers and providing and maintaining software for the computers. Every department in this information firm utilizes computers including the department in which Darla works.

Darla has been with the company only six months. When she was hired, it took almost three weeks to get a computer on her desk. When she did receive the computer, it lacked the proper software to interface with the rest of DCI and customers. Though Buelah's computer-support unit is just on the other side of Darla's cubicle, Darla was told she had to wait a few weeks before getting the proper software. After getting the software, she was unsure how to use it properly. When Darla asked Buelah's staff about the software operation, she received unclear and demeaning responses.

About three months ago, Darla and a co-worker requested laptop computers for work while they're traveling. Their immediate manager, S. Temple approved the request. During the next three weeks, Darla repeatedly asked members of Buelah's staff when she'd get her laptop computer. The staff verified that the computers were in stock but that Darla had to wait until the proper channels were cleared. They added, "You should do less complaining." Efforts to solicit help from Temple, her manager, brought no useful responses.

Darla happens to live close to B. Shot, so she decided one day to stop and discuss the problem away from the work setting. B. Shot told Darla, "I don't get involved in these problems. The units have to resolve their own conflicts. Go talk to your unit manager." So Darla went back to Temple with the problem. Temple said, "I don't want to get Buelah mad or we'll get less computer support than we get now."

Two weeks ago, Darla couldn't get her computer to print. She had to call the computer-support department to get it fixed. She was frustrated about not getting her work done with the computer down. After three days of calls and lack of response, Darla sent a memo to Buelah with a copy to B. Shot. It said, "In order to get my work done, please help me with this computer problem."

Buelah flashed the memo around the department while labeling Darla as a complainer. Darla said at this point, "We do everything we can for the computer-support unit, yet they don't do a thing to make our job easier. They just don't get the big picture. They lack consideration and the commitment to cooperate!" After the third day, Darla found someone else in the department who helped her resolve the printing problem.

After a little investigation, Darla found out that B. Shot had promoted Buelah to the head of her department about a year ago, based primarily on Buelah's technical expertise. Darla also found that her unit's previous manager, P. Weakly had quit because he disliked confronting other managers in order to get support for some of his unit's tasks.

Darla is concerned that if she went to Human Resources, she'd be further labeled as a complainer, especially since neither B. Shot or S. Temple will support her. Yet she is bothered that her work is hampered by lack of computer support.

1. What strategy should Darla use to approach her problems with the computer support unit?

2. If other units have similar problems and we can assume that Buelah's unit is not going to change, what do workers for DCI need to do to make this a manageable situation?

CHAPTER TEN

Learning Individuals in Learning Organizations

We have achieved and will continue to achieve dramatic progress through people who are perpetual learners, people who are skilled in the application of that learning, people who are committed to the application of these skills in the improvement of their company.

John Towers (1996), CEO of Rover Group
Largest Car Manufacturer in England

Joe is a labor negotiator who works for a large manufacturing firm. Before becoming a representative, he worked in factory jobs for almost 20 years. Despite his lack of a college education Joe is proud of his achievements as a leader. His style is brusque, tough and direct. Today he has a meeting with a representative from management. After conversing with the workers he represents, he decided to adopt a firm, unbending stance in today's negotiation.

Sean is the corporate negotiator who represents management. His university education includes a graduate degree in law. Sean has never worked in a factory. He prides himself on his rhetoric skills and meticulously crafts everything he says. After meeting with the group he represents, like Joe, Sean has decided to adopt a firm, unbending stance with regard to the issues.

As the meeting progresses, discussion is predictable. Both Joe and Sean engage in selective listening, filtering out information that doesn't match with their group's perspective. Both men hide more information than they share, and distort the meaning of the other's words. They both look for reasons to oppose agreement. The meeting ends without resolution of the problems; however, they agree to meet again the next day.

That evening as Sean sat at the dinner table, his 16-year old son, asked about taking a trip with his friends next weekend. Sean bristled, and linked the discussion to homework that hadn't been completed, to unfinished chores, and his son's "disrespectful" comments. His son stormed away from the table, frustrated with his father's lack of understanding.

Later that night, Sean commented to his wife, "There has to be a better way. Conversations and relationships like the ones I've had today are wearing me out." The chasm between Sean and his son is very similar to the chasm at work between Sean and Joe. Opposing viewpoints and conflicting needs require a communication bridge that shows understanding. Sean failed at creating communication bridges, both at home and at work. After his discussion with his wife, he decided to try some different tactics, with both his son and the labor committee representative.

The next day, Joe expected the same, self-centered, unbending stance from Sean. He didn't get it. Sean began asking questions that demonstrated a desire to understand. His statements displayed respect for the interests and expertise of the labor negotiator. When discussing difficult issues he took a perspective that the relationship mattered as much as the decisions. The day before, Joe's statements triggered angry responses, but today Sean remained neutral and issue-focused. As the day went on, Joe softened his tough stance and became more flexible on the issues that separated them. Eventually they agreed on a proposal they would each take back to their groups for approval. At the end of the work day, Sean said to a colleague, "Maybe it's time to try the same communication style at home with my son." He decided that he would begin with doing more warm-up. He'd ask about his son's day. He'd focus more on listening and would respect the things his son valued. He would try to emphasize similarities before turning to differences and would work harder to understand the situation before making decisions.

Sean's problems are similar to those encountered daily in organizational, family, and social settings. Cultural background and gender issues frequently complicate the communication struggles. Liska and Cronkhite (1995) suggest,

> *We need to maintain a tolerant and open point of view in which we recognize that cultural differences result from the fact that different people have solved problems in the best way they can, given the circumstances of their history and the environment which they live. (397)*

Effective communication begins when we build bridges between different perspectives and cultural understandings. The following list summarizes many of the communication skills that accomplish this goal.

Communication Bridges	Example
Listen with the goal of understanding	Help me understand
Demonstrate concern for the interests and needs of others	How can I help you accomplish your goals?
Respect the perspective of others, even if we don't agree	I value your opinion
Clarify the meaning of statements instead of jumping to conclusions	Let me see if I understand correctly
Relate to others with an attitude of humility	I certainly could be wrong here
Manage the stress we bring to the situation	It's not you today, I'm just tired
Prevent issues of pride and ego from getting in the way of building relationships	I'm sorry if I let my stubbornness get in the way of resolving differences
Understand that our unintentional messages may at times overshadow our intentional messages	Let me clarify what I mean because I don't think it's coming across clearly
Communicate openness to feedback, avoid getting defensive	I appreciate your comments. What else do you think we could do?
Create an emotional climate of safety, trust, and respect	I want you to know you can talk to me without being attacked

We live in an era of frequent changes that impact the settings where we form relationships. Adapting our communication to meet the situational needs will improve our success with relationships. Sean's willingness to promote understanding with his son, will probably influence his quality of life at home. Anything less will recycle his frustrations. Wilson Learning Laboratories identified *flexibility* and *adaptability* as the most important communication skills needed in the next decade. New technologies professors, Johansen and Swigart (1996) identify a few of the cultural changes that are creating the need:

- Organizations are evolving from pyramid to fishnet structures as hierarchies collapse and broad, interwoven, flexible structures emerge.
- Within organizations, individuals are less apt to work in big structures and more likely to participate in business teams and ad hoc alliances.
- Electronic networks are replacing office buildings as the locus of business transactions.
- Climbing the organizational hierarchy is no longer like climbing stairs in a stable structure. The stairs have become rope ladders, with managers clinging desperately for balance, (p. 6-8).

Learning organizations

The ability to adapt communication processes in order to meet changing organizational demands has given rise to the concept of learning organizations.

Companies that function as learning organizations focus on "generative learning, or creating, as well as adaptive learning, or coping" (Senge, 1990, p. 8). Mohrman and Mohrman (1993) describe the dynamics of learning organizations,

> *Learning occurs when the organization is able to respond to environmental change by adding new patterns of activity, deleting patterns that are not needed and/or by developing better sensing mechanisms that allow the appropriate matching of activity to particular environmental events (p. 89).*

Accountability for organizational success must be shared by the employees. Interpersonal skills need to guide organizational problem solving and decision making. Eugene Dilbreck, president of the Denver Metro Convention and Tourist Bureau identifies the priorities as, "We must be able to admit our own vulnerabilities, turn our rejections around, and encourage our strengths." Top to bottom, members must seek to transform, create, and re-invent efficient processes for organizational success. Research indicates that only about 3% of all organizations have reached the level of being a learning organization.

In the early 1980's, Shell Oil was one of the first companies to include learning organizational principles in their strategic planning. Since then, similar principles have been adopted by Maxwell House, General Electric, Pacific Bell, Quad Graphics, Federal Express, Ford, Corning, Motorola, Honda, and Samsung. As companies attempt to evolve into learning organizations, they must develop a consistent set of goals:

- View the organization as a system in which each of the parts affect the whole
- Place high value on innovation and creativity
- Create a flexible structure that's responsive to innovation
- Help workers feel empowered and responsible for innovative change
- Develop, maintain, and enhance core competencies
- Continuously re-invent work processes to make them more effective.

Key words in this set of characteristics include *innovative, creative, flexible* and *responsive*. These are the same characteristics that Sean needed in order to relate more effectively in both his negotiation at work and problem solving with his teenage son.

Learning organizations effectively manage the acquisition, storage, distribution, and interpretation of information. Sean's experience paralleled this as he became more focused in his listening (acquired information), engaged in respectful discussion (distribution), and negotiated a common understanding (interpretation). Learning organizations seek to improve the processes by which information is shared and utilized.

University of Texas business administration professors George Huber and William Glick (1993) suggest that learning organizations need:

- Decision making processes that are more frequent, effective and complex
- Information acquisition that is continuous and wide ranging
- Rapid implementation of decisions
- Directed distribution of information
- Intentionally managed organizational learning (p. 8)

A learning organization's effectiveness will depend on workers' ability to adapt to these changing needs. Professor of Organizational Behavior at George Washington University, Michael Marquardt proposes that "Learning should be occurring as an automatic and integral part of production, marketing, problem solving, finance, customer service, and every other aspect of the company" (p. 185).

Challenges of perception

Robert Mai, vice president of Performance Improvement Company, points out that learning organizations will not fully develop until they are able to overcome problems with perceptions. Sometimes becoming a learning organization is limited by the perceptions of key employees.

Perception Problems

• Tunnel vision	Unwillingness to look at the big picture and how individual behaviors might influence the greater organization
• Myopic vision	Inability or unwillingness to see beyond the day-to-day deadlines and demands
• Blind spot vision	Difficulty recognizing or understanding the problems of others

---

These perceptions create communication challenges similar to dealing with difficult people or difficult situations. Learning organizations require members who are able to widen their perceptions to include a greater diversity of ideas, agendas, and goals. Open-mindedness, perseverance and communication skills determine the limits for how effective a group will be in achieving goals or managing complex tasks. Organizational consultants Boyett and Conn (1991) predict, "Every American business and every employee who works for an American business will be forced to become agile, flexible, and highly adaptive since...the business processes they employ will be in a constant state of change" (p. xiii).

Nadler et al., (1992) identify two additional requirements for groups to become learning settings. Workers must be confident that there are a sufficient number of people working for a more collaborative climate. People will not communicate openly and fully if they feel powerless to make things happen. Organizations often require a champion in management who says, "This is where we're going and I'll make it happen."

Secondly, workers must be highly committed to a new way of doing things. People find it difficult to engage in collaborative learning processes if their jobs have too many priorities. Expending additional effort on team meetings, innovative approaches, or checking with someone before making a decision may require more energy and time than they're willing to invest. Creating processes that build a learning organization may require simplifying and clarifying work roles to help build commitment to change.

A major midwestern corporation operated nationally under the direction of a CEO and seven vice presidents. One of the vice presidents believed that to be competitive in the market, decisions needed to be rigorously discussed by many levels of management before being implemented. He formed groups of 10-15 people whose task was to critically examine current decisions and evaluate innovative possibilities. These "futuristic teams" initially had support from the six other vice presidents. Quarterly, the group members flew in from five states to participate in decision-making discussions. After 18 months, the groups were disbanded and the vice president resigned to move to another company. Insiders said, "His approach was too controversial. The other staff weren't comfortable with major decisions being discussed so openly." Having a champion in management does not guarantee success with accomplishing change. Innovative processes that involve sharing of confidential information and collaborating on decisions may be limited by wider organizational issues.

Learning Organizations	Stagnant Organizations
• People are open to and welcome feedback	• People closed to feedback
• People seek best solution	• People seek to be right, to win
• Collaborative mindset	• Competitive mindset
• Mistakes are opportunities to learn	• Mistakes are to be avoided
• High risk taking	• High risk avoidance
• People take responsibility	• People tend to blame one another
• Strong spirit of shared ownership	• Strong sense of dependence
• Change is welcomed	• Change is avoided
• Strong sense of purpose	• Overemphasis on immediate results

(Source: Keith Marron, *Riding the Wave*, 1995, p.404)

Learning individuals

Learning settings, whether in organizations or families, require individuals who possess the receptivity and intent to be continuous learners. In organizations where problems are continually recycling or escalating, we usually hear "They're just not willing to change how they do things." Unwillingness to recognize ineffective processes or weak listening skills creates cycles with negative outcomes. When Sean acknowledged that his communication tactics were ineffective, he changed his approach and achieved success with Joe as well as his son.

Learning organizations require management and staff who accept responsibility for creating and maintaining effective procedures. Organizations learn only through individuals who learn. Senge (1990) suggests that, "Individual learning does not guarantee organizational learning, but without it, no organizational learning occurs" (p. 236). In 1991, the US Secretary of Labor, Robert Reich, commissioned a group to predict the communication skills required of workers in the year 2000. The group, called the Secretary's Commission on Achieving Necessary Skills for the American Workplace, issued a report that recommended the following priorities:

- Understand their work in the context of the work around them
- Monitor and correct their own problems
- Negotiate with others to solve problems or reach decisions
- Identify, assimilate and integrate information from different sources
- Develop strategies for accomplishing team objectives and resolving group conflict
- Work well with people from a variety of ethnic, social, or educational backgrounds

(Source: Boyette, 1995)

The competencies that encourage personal responsibility for learning are based on an attitude of discovery. Employees need a strong capacity to rebound from disappointment, ability to recognize choices for improving interactions and willingness to share what they know.

Personal responsibilities

A learning individual accepts personal responsibility for organizational communication dynamics. Too often people see their role as someone who points out problems with people and systems. But a learning individual accepts responsibility for contributions to the dynamics. Harvard professor Chris Argyris (1996) suggests, "They need to reflect critically on their own behaviors, identify the way they often and inadvertently contribute to the organization's problems, and then change the way they act" (p. 84).

In 1991, *Life Magazine* listed Billy Jean King as one of the top 100 most respected Americans of the 20th century. In response to questions about her success, King said, "It's learning about your craft...It's about decisions, corrections, choices. I don't think it's so much about becoming a tennis player. It's about becoming a person" (Jenkins, 1991, 72). In terms of organizational communication, learning individuals attempt to understand the impact of their communication choices on co-workers and team processes. This includes a conscious decision to examine our own actions and a willingness to change the choices we make in our interpersonal communication.

Communication choice

Communication processes involve a sequence of *choices.* My message to you triggers a thought or feeling. You hear my message, interpret the meaning, and send back a message, which in turn triggers thoughts and feelings in me. We engage in a series of transactions which influence the flow of meaning and direction of conversation. If we're in a group, the dynamics are multiplied. A single message can trigger responses in several people at one time, anything from contagious enthusiasm to defensiveness.

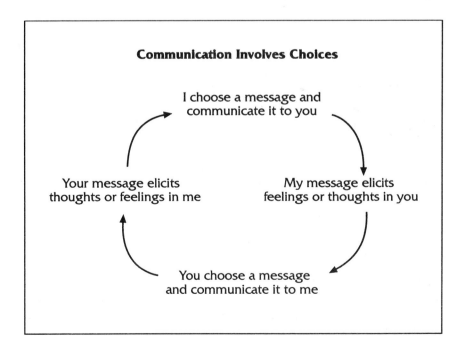

Communication Involves Choices

I choose a message and communicate it to you

My message elicits feelings or thoughts in you

You choose a message and communicate it to me

Your message elicits thoughts or feelings in me

Attitude of discovery

The learning individual approaches communication with an attitude of discovery. Marquardt (1996) describes this priority as "free and creative exploration of subtle issues" (p. 46). An attitude of discovery involves asking questions that promote understanding instead of advancing arguments. As a tool for discovery, questioning accomplishes many purposes:

- Help focus our thoughts
- Bridge conflicting views by identifying common ground
- Strengthen relationships by demonstrating concern
- Deflect attacks by seeking more understanding
- Turn discomforting silence into clarifying discourse
- Convey subtle messages that imply rather than assert

(Source: Deep & Susskind, 1993)

Discovery involves *multiframe thinking* where people choose to view organizational issues from many perspectives (Bolman & Deal, 1991). To view an issue as singular in its cause oversimplifies complex relationships. We enhance understanding when we allow for the possibility that there are many subtle but significant considerations underlying problems.

Questioning, as a tool of inquiry, must include sensitivity to those being questioned. People become defensive if you threaten the way they do things. Questioning involves more listening than speaking and being sensitive to egos and needs. The goal is understanding, not destruction. Inquiry, or seeking to understand, is balanced with advocacy, or arguing on behalf of an idea or proposal.

Discovery is forward looking. Too often organizations get preoccupied with what was done in the past, and drain their energy for dealing with the present. Oakley & Krug (1991) use the term *energy ratio* to describe how we invest energy. Devoting too much energy to studying the past creates attitudes such as, "We can't do anything" or "Nothing ever changes." In the proper balance, future-directed focus can energize groups.

Looking backward	Looking forward
Blame others for not fixing emotion	Focus on solutions
Rehearsing past failures	Emphasizing opportunities
High "whine" factor	Minimizing complaining
Defensive orientation	Solution-focused orientation
Focusing on how things used to be	Learning to adapt to change
Preoccupied with emotions, such as anger	Able to step back from emotions and look at big picture

On every issue and in every relationship, we have choices about where to invest our energy. An attitude of discovery focuses the greater share of energy on "How can we fix this?" "What new processes do we need," or "How can this be prevented?"

Rebound factor

The development of learning organizations requires workers who have a strong capacity to rebound from disappointment. In our work we have often described this as the *rebound factor*. Some individuals have a great capacity to overcome roadblocks to achieve success. Others give up after a single attempt at something. Some examples of people with a strong rebound factor in their learning style are:

- Henry Ford went broke five times before he finally succeeded.
- Thomas Edison's father called him a "dunce" and predicted that he "would never make a success of anything." Thomas didn't allow these words to get in the way of his career.
- Charles Darwin failed a medical school course at Edinburg's University and barely passed his classes at Cambridge.
- Eighteen publishers turned down Richard Bach's 10,000 word essay about a "soaring seagull." Yet by the early 1970s, his book, Jonathon Livingston Seagull, had sold over seven million copies for MacMillan.

- A teacher advised Albert Einstein to drop out of school because the only subject he was good at was math. Later, Einstein even failed the entrance exam at Zurich's Polytechnic Institute. His failures did not overcome his ability to continue learning and be successful.
- The humorous Korean war novel, M•A•S•H, was a seven year project for Richard Hooker, and was initially turned down by 21 publishers.

Learning individuals who are successful in organizations are determined, persistent, and committed to new and better ways to get things done. B.C. Forbes, founder of *Forbes Magazine*, said, "One worthwhile task is better than half-a-hundred half-finished tasks" (Quebin, 1983, p. 27).

Following the 1983 American recession, James Houghton, CEO of Corning Inc., described the mood of his workers as "mired deep in the mud and we had to do something different" (Wick & Leon, 1993, p. 12). Their rebound began with a two-day institute on innovation. They formed a committee whose goal was to institutionalize innovative processes. It took five years of strategic planning, but they became a learning organization. The ability to rebound is a characteristic of successful learners, individually and organizationally. Integral to these processes is a group of learners who engage in dialogue without defensiveness and negotiate new understandings.

A learning individual is sensitive to the sequences that build communication patterns. When destructive sequences continue, their communication must be changed to break the pattern. The adaptive communicator is continuously monitoring communication to identify messages that are effective and ones that cause problems.

Stewart (1993) conducted a study that looked at the formal and informal communication patterns in team settings. He found that miscommunication most often occurred in one of four ways:

- Workers sent inappropriate information
- Workers disregarded important information
- Workers communicated too little information
- Workers communicated with insufficient respect for co-worker

Organizational communication involves a continual effort to adapt communication in a way that achieves a balance between to much and too little. Destructive cycles can be recognized by statements such as, "I didn't know," "Why wasn't I informed of this?" or "Why are you telling me? What am I supposed to do about it?" When speakers monologue for too long a time, sharing every aspect of a situation and everything tangential to it, they may unknowingly create responses of boredom or indifference. Listeners quit listening and caring long before the speaker is finished.

The adaptive communicator constructs messages that are sensitive to situational needs and to the feelings and beliefs of listeners. Learning individuals become keen observers of how well their messages achieve their goals. They continually reshape, re-invent, and adapt communication to make it effective.

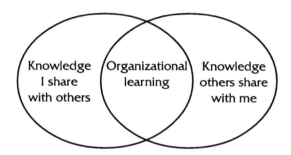

Collective meaning

Learning in organizations is an active social phenomenon and a partnership. Studies at the Institute for Research and Learning in Palo Alto, California found that people learn the most when they belong to "overlapping communities of practice with differing specialties" (Johansen & Swigart, 1996, p. 136). Individual learning contributes to collective learning as members add their knowledge to the efforts to find better ways to do things. Dixon (1994) describes the group's combined knowledge as *collective meaning*. As the group collaboratively agrees on norms, strategies, and assumptions, collective meaning occurs. These agreements guide how work gets divided and how tasks are performed. *My way* is replaced with *our way*. The goal is to tap the collective intelligence of the group. Investing energy in groups serves many purposes. For example, project groups provide opportunity to:

- Create an interpersonal network that provides resources for solving day-to-day problems
- Understand how our issues relate to the larger issues of the organization
- Test the value of options
- Transfer knowledge and skills among the group's members
- Develop shared understandings that might make procedures more predictable
- Draw on a wider range of knowledge for complex problems

Our wisdom with the group and being open to wisdom shared by others involves the intersection of individual learning with organizational learning.

Learning groups

Organizations are utilizing the benefits of interactive learning that occurs in teams or in groups. Based on recommendations that came from groups, 3M found that they could cut unit costs by 10%, cut the manufacturing cycle time by 50%, and reduce development time for new products (Kelly, 1991). Many companies, such as AT&T, General Mills, Goodyear Tire, and Ford Motor Company claim that higher quality or greater productivity occurred as a result of a team-based approach.

For individual learning to occur in the group context, members need to approach discussions non-defensively and with openness to the ideas of others. "Our ability to learn...is determined by the quality and openness of our relationships" (Marquardt, 1996, p. 31). Group members who have already "made up their mind," rarely learn nor do they create a climate where others want to learn from them. Communication that facilitates both individual and organizational learning and includes :

- Separate ego from ideas, and take a creative, less reactive stance
- Suspend certainty so that all possibilities can be critically examined
- Respect the opinions and contributions of others
- Approach the issues with an attitude of discovery
- Resist the desire to monologue about the issues. Foster a climate of dialogue.

In organizations, much of our group communication focuses on problem solving and decision making. We bring dilemmas to our project teams and we look for insights or better ways to manage them. We ask groups for input about how to handle a sensitive situation. We are learners with a goal of discovery. But groups are not always the most effective context in which to discuss issues. Occasionally, many people walk away from a meeting saying, "I wish I hadn't brought that subject up" or "It would have been simpler to do it myself." Discussions that unnecessarily escalate tension may have a negative impact on relationships and on the quality of the organizational climate. Asking for input from group member who lack knowledge of the issue may frustrate them rather than make them feel included.

Kreps (1990) provides a set of criteria for knowing whether to discuss a problem in the group or whether to handle it individually:

Group solutions are best	Individual solutions are best
If the problem is impersonal	If the problem is personal
If the problem is of moderate difficulty	If the problem is simple
If several people are needed to provide the information to solve the problem	If information to solve the problem can be provided by one person
If the problem requires several solutions	If the problem requires just one solution
If a great deal of time is required for solution of the problem	If a small amount of time is required for solution of the problem
If attitudes regarding the problem are going to be many and complex	If attitudes toward the problem are going to be simple. (p. 174)

The learning organization of the future

Becoming a learning organization or an effective team requires people who have strong interpersonal skills. Communicating with clarity, listening longer, and negotiating our differences help us to meet organizational challenges. When problems are complex or situations especially difficult, progress will be measured by incremental steps rather than big changes. By focusing on a spirit of collaboration, we make a major contribution to the development of learning organizations.

In *The Sneetches*, Dr. Seuss describes two stubborn Zaks who refuse to alter the paths they're walking even though they're going to bump into each other. As they stand nose to nose, Dr. Seuss writes,

*'Not an inch to the West. Not an inch to the East. I'll stay here,
not budging, I can and I will. If it makes you and me and the
whole world stand still'...Of course the world didn't stand
still...the world grew...and left them there, standing
unbudged in their tracks. (32, 35)*

We are like the Zaks. We can stay where we are, unbudging in the way
we do things, but the world will keep moving and changing. It will leave
us behind unless we adapt. Our communication skills will be the vehicle
for our success as we move forward into the next century.

References

Adler, R. (1986). *Communicating at work*. New York: Random House.

Adler, R.B. & Rodman, G. (1994). *Understanding human communication*. Fort Worth: Holt, Rinehart & Winston.

Adler, R.B., Rosenfeld, L. B. & Towne, N. (1989). *Interplay*. New York: Holt, Rinehart, and Winston.

Adler, R.B., & Towne, N. (1996). *Looking out/looking in: Interpersonal communication* (8th ed.) Fort Worth: Harcourt Brace.

Adrian, P. (1994, August). From the editor: Managing human resources is vital for successful manufacturing. *Manufacturing Automaton*, 3 (11), [paragraph 3, electronic].

Albrecht, T.L. (1982). Coping with occupational stress: Relational and individual strategies of nurses in acute health care settings. In M. Burgoon (Ed.) *Communication Yearbook*, 6, 1982.

Alderson, S.(1993). Reframing management competence: Focusing on the top management teams. *Personnel Review*, 22 (6), 53-62.

Anderson, K. (1993). *Getting what you want*. New York: Dutton.

Andrews, P. & Herschel, R.T. (1996). *Organizational communication*. *Boston: Houghton Mifflin.*

Argyris, C. (1993). Skilled incompetence. In *Articulate Executive* (17-28). Boston: Harvard Business Review.

Argyris, C. (July/August, 1996). Good communication that blocks learning. Harvard Business Review, 77-85.

Augsburger, D. (1982). Caring enough to hear and be heard. Scottsdale, PA: Herald Press.

Axrelrod, R. (1984). *The evolution of cooperation*. New York: Basic Books.

Bach, G. & Deutsch, R. (1979) *Stop! You're driving me crazy*. New York: Berkeley Books.

Badawy, M. K. (August, 1994). Getting the most from a cross-functional team: Management. *Electronic Business Buyer*, 20 (8), 65.

Baker, W. E. (1994). *Networking smart*. New York: McGraw-Hill.

Barbour, A. (1995). Unpublished raw data.

Baron, J. N. & Pfeffer, J. (1994). The social psychology of organizations and inequality. *Social Psychology Quarterly*, 57 (3), 190-209.

Bartolome, F. (1993). Nobody trusts the boss - Now what? In *Articulate Executive* (3-16). Boston: Harvard Business Review.

Bastien, D. T. (1987). Common patterns of behavior and communication in corporate mergers and acquisitions. *Human Resource Management*, 26 (1), 17-33.

Bazerman, M. H. & Neale, M. A. (1992). *Negotiating rationally*. New York: The Free Press.

Becker, E. (1971). *The birth and death of meaning*. Free Press: New York.

Bennett, A. (1991, June 6). Downsizing doesn't necessarily bring an upswing in corporate prfitability. *Wall Street Journal*, p. B1.

Bennett, J.C. & Olney, R.J. (1986). Executive priorities for effective communication in the information society. *The Journal of Business Communication, 23*, 13-22.

Berelson, B. and Steiner, G.A. (1964). *Human behavior: An inventory of scientific findings*. New York: Harcourt Brace Jovanovich.

Bolman, L G. & Deal, T.E. (1991). *Reframing organizations*. San Francisco: Jossey-Bass.

Boyette, J. H. and Conn, H. P. (1991). *Workplace 2000: The revolution reshaping American businesses*. New York: NAL/Dutton.

Boyette, J. H. (1995). *Beyond Workplace 2000: Essential strategies for the new corporation. New York: Dutton.*

Braham, J. (1993). Building a winning team. *Machine Design, 65* (24), 74-76.

Bramson, R. (1981). *Coping with difficult people*. New York: Ballantine.

Brown, C. T. & Van Riper, C. V. (1981). The role of speech in human relationships. In B. R. Patton & K. Giffin (Eds.) *Interpersonal Communication in Action* (338-347). New York: Harper and Row.

Burgoon, J. K., & Hale, J. L. (1987). Validation and measurement of the fundamental themes of relational communication. *Communication Monographs, 54*, 19-41.

Burgoon, J. K., Buller, D. B. & Woodall, W. G. (1989). *Nonverbal communication: The unspoken dialogue*. New York: Harper & Row.

Campbell, S. (1995). *The chaos of change*. New Yor: Simon and Shuster.

Castro, J. (1993, March 29). Disposable workers, *Time*.

Cava, R. (1990). *Difficult people*. Toronto, Canada: Key Porter.

Clawson, J. G. (1989). You can't manage them if they don't trust you. *Executive Excellence, 6* (4), 10-11.

Cottrell, R. and Robertson, C.J. (1987, September). The HRIS profession: Development and direction. *Personnel Journal, 66* (9), 11-120.

Coule, M. B. (1993). Quality interpersonal communication - An overview. *Manage,44* (4), 4-5.

Cronkite, G. (1976). *Communication and awareness*. Menlo Park, CA: Benjamin.

Curtin, L. L. (1993). Doing the right thing. *Nursing Management, 24* (12), 17-19.

Cusella, L.P. (1987). Feedback,motivation, and performance. In F. M. Jablin, L.L. Putman, K. H.
Roberts, & L. W. Porter (Eds.) *Handbook of organizational communication* (pp. 624-678). Newbury Park, CA: Sage.

Cushman, D. & Cahn, D.(1985). *Communication in interpersonal relationships*. Albany, NY: State University of New York Press.

Daft, R.L., Bettenhausen, K., & Tyler, B. (1993). Implications of top managers' communication choices for strategic decisions. In G. Glick and W. Glick (Eds.) *Organizational change and redesign (pp. 112- 146)*. New York: Oxford University.

Davis, K. (1988). "Management Communication and the grapevine. *Harvard Business Review, 31*, 43-49.

Deal, T. and Kennedy, A. (1982). *Corporate cultures: The rites and rituals of corporate life*. Reading, MA: Adison-Wesley.

Deep, S. and Sussman, L. (1993). *What to ask when you don't know what to say.* Englewood Cliffs, N J: Prentice Hall.

Dixon, N. (1994). *The organizational learning cycle.* London: McGraw-Hill.

Dr. Seuss, (1961). *The Sneetches.* New York: Random House.

Dumaine, B. (1989, February 3). How managers can succeed through speed. *Fortune,* 54-59.

Eisenberg, E. M. & Goodall, H. L. (1993). *Organizational communication: Balancing creativity and constraint.* New York: St. Martin's Press.

Fisher,R., Kopelman, E. & Schneider, A.K. (1994). *Beyond Machiavelli.* Cambridge: Harvard University.

Floyd, J.J. (1985). *Listening: A practical approach.* Glenview, IL: Scott, Foresman.

Fortune de Felice (1976). Negotiations or the art of negotiating. In W. Zartman (Ed.) *The 50% solution* (pp. 56). New Haven: Yale University Press.

Gibb, J. (1961). Defensive communication. *Journal of Communication,* 11 (3), 142-148.

Goss B. & O'Hair, D. (1988). Communicating in interpersonal relationships. New York: MacMillan Publishing Company.

Gordon, R.D. (1988). The difference between feeling defensive and feeling understood. *The Journal of Business Communication,* 25, 53-64.

Gouthro, D. (1991,). Dealing with difficult people. *Performance and Instruction,* 30 (5), 11-12.

Grice, P. (1975). *Studies in the way of words.* Cambridge, Massachusetts: Harvard University.

Haney, W. V. (1973). *Communication and organizational behavior.* Homewood, Illinois: Irwin.

Harris, T. (1993). *Applied organizational communication.* Hillsdale, NJ: Lawrence Erlbaum Associates.

Hass, N. (1995, October 30). Grab something to eat . . . it's free! *U. S. News & World Report,* 119 (17), Special Supplement.

Hayakawa, S. I. (1964). *Language in thought and action.* New York: Harcourt Brace.

Heckel, N. (1987). Communication skills training comes of age. *Training and Development Journal,* 41 (7), 72-73.

Hellweg, (1987). Organizational grapevine: A state of the art review. In B. Dervin & M.J. Voight (Eds.) *Progress in Communication Sciences Volume 8* (pp. 213-230). Norwood: Ablex.

Henkoff, R. (1990). Cost cutting. How to do it right. *Fortune,* 27, 40-47.

Hill, G. W. (1982). Group vs individual performance: Are N + 1 better than one? *Psychological Bulletin,* 91, 517-539.

Hollwitz, J., Churchill, R., & Hollwitz, T. (1985). Communication with the difficult personality: Adaptive responses in organizational settings. Paper presented to the annual convention of theSpeech Communication Association, Washington, D.C.

Huber, G. P. and Glick, W. H. (1993). Sources as forms of organizational change. In G.P. Huber and W.H. Glick (Eds.) *Organizational change and redesign* (pp. 3-15). New York: Oxford.

Iacocca, L. (1984). *Iacocca: An autobiography.* New York: Bantam Books.

Infante, D.A. & Gorden, W.I. (1985). Superiors' argumentativeness and verbal aggressiveness as predictors of subordinates' satisfaction. *Human Communication Research*, 12, 117-125.

Infante, D.A. & Gorden, W.I. (1989). Argumentativeness and affirming communicator style as predictors of satisfaction/dissatisfaction with subordinates. *Communication Quarterly*, 37,81-90.

Infante, D. A., Rancer, A. S., & Womack, D.F. (1990). *Building communication theory*. Prospect Heights, ILL: Waveland Press.

Jablin, F. (1979). Superior-subordinate communication: The state of the art. *Psychological Bulletin*, 86 (6), 201-1222.

Jenkins, S. (1991, April 29). Raquet science. *Sports Illustrated*, p. 72.

Johansen, R. & Swigart, R. (1996). *Upsizing the individual in the downsized organization*. Reading, Mass: Addison-Wesley.

Johnson, D. W. & Johnson, R. T. (1989). *Cooperation and conflict: Theory and research*. Edina, MN: Interaction Book Company.

Johnson, V. (1992). Two-person interactions: Trifle or treasure? *Successful Meetings*, 41(13), 128-129.

Johnsson, J. (1992). Openness is the key to trustee bonding. *Hospitals*, 66 (13), 152.

Kelly, K. (1991, Sept 16). 3M run scared? Forget about it. *Business Week*, p. 59, 62.

Kemp, K.E. & Smith, W.P. (1994). Information exchange, toughness, and integrative bargaining: The roles of explicit cues and perspective-taking. *The International Journal of Conflict Management*, 5 (1), 5-21.

Keys, B. and Case, T. (1990). How to become an influencial manager. *Academy of Management Executive*, 4, 38-50.

Keyser, T. (1994). *Teampower*. Burr Ridge, ILL: Irwin.

Kikoski, J. F. (1993, Spring). Effective communication in the intranational workplace: Models for public sectors managers and theorists. *Public Administration Quarterly*, 17 (1), 84-95.

Kinlaw, D.C. (1991). *Developing superior work teams: Building quality and the competitive edge*. Lexington, MA: Lexington Books.

Koermer, C. Goldstein, M. & Fortson, D. (1993). How supervisers communicatively convey immediacy to subordinates An exploratory qualitative investigation. *Eastern Communication Journal*, 41, 269-281.

Kohli, A. K., & Jaworski, B. J. (1994). The influence of coworker feedback on salespeople. *Journal of Marketing*, 58, 82-94.

Krackhardt, D. (1990). Assessing the political landscape: Structure, cognition, and power ing organizations. *Administrative Science Quarterly*, 35, 342-369.

Kreps, G. (1990). *Organizational Communication*. New York: Longman.

Lamuda, K.G., Daniels, T.D. & Graham, E.E. (1988). The paradoxical influence of sex on communication rules coorientation and communication satisfaction in superior-subordinate relationships. *Western Journal of Speech Communication*, 52, 122-134.

Lamuda, K.G., Scudder, J. & Dickson, R. (1993). Relational communication messges of Type-A scoring physicians. *Perceptual and Motor Skills*, 77 (3), 985-986.

Larson, C. (1995). Meta-analysis empirical and relational factors in 100 team communication studies. Unpublished raw data.

Larson, C.E. & LeFasto, F.M. (1989). *TeamWork*. Newbury Park: Sage.

Lashbrook, W. & Lashbrook V. (1975). *A computer analysis of small group communication*. Minneapolis: Burgess.

Lawrence, P.R. & Lorsch, J.W. (1976). *Organization and environment*. Homewood, IL: Irwin.

Level, D.A. (1972). Communication effectiveness: Method and situation. *Journal of Business Communication*, 10, 19-25.

Liska, J. & Cronkhite, G. (1995). *An ecological perspective on human communication theory*. Fort Worth: Harcourt Brace.

Lombardo, M. & McCall, M. (1984, January). Intolerable boss. *Psychology Today*, p.45-48.

London, M., & Beatty, R. W. (1993). 360-degree feedback as a competitive advantage. *Human Resource Management*, 32 , 353-372.

Maier, N. (1967). Assets and liabilities in group problem solving. *Psychological Review*,74, 239-249.

Managers, listen or lose best workers (1987, July 7). USA Today, p. 4B.

Manning, G. & Curtis, K. (1988). *Communication: The miracle of dialogue*. Cincinnati: South-Western.

Marquardt, M. (1996). *Building the learning organization*. New York: McGraw-Hill.

Marron, K. (1995) *Riding the Wave*. New York: Van Nostrand Reinhold.

McCann, J.E. & Selsky, J. (1984). Hyperturbulence and the emergence of type 5 environments. *Academy of Management Review*, 9, 460-470.

McLeod, P. L. (1992). An assessment of the experimental literature on electronic support group work: Results of a meta-analysis. *Human Computer Interaction*, 7(3), 257-280.

Mehrebian, A. & Weiner, M. (1967). Decoding of inconsistent communications. *Journal of Personality and Social Psychology*, 6, 109-114.

Mintzberg, H. (1983). The managers job: Folklore and fact. In K. Andrews (Ed.) *Executive success: Making it in management* (pp. 414-435). New York: John Wiley and Sons.

Monroe, C., Borzi, M., & DiSalvo, V. (1989). Conflict behaviors of difficult subordinates. *Southern Communication Journal*, 54, 311-329.

Moorhead, J.A. (1991). Co-orientation in relational themes, satisfaction, and conflict interactins: The study of marital and organizational peer dialogues. Unpublished dissertation, University of Denver.

Nadler, D.A., Gerstein, M., & Shaw, P. (1992). *Organizational architecture: Design for changing organizations*. San Francisco: Jossey-Bass.

Nemeth, C. J. & Kwan, J. L. (1987). Minority influence, divergent thinking and detection of correct solutions. *Journal of Applied Social Psychology*, 17, 788-799.

Newman, R. G. (1990). Polaroid develops a communication system - but not instantly. *Management Review*, 79 (1), 34-38.

O'Conaill, B., Whittaker, S., & Wilbur, S. (1993). Conversations over video conferences: An evaluation of the spoken aspects of video-mediated communication. *Human Computer Interaction*, 8 (4), 389-428.

Oakley, E. & Krug, D. (1991). *Enlightened leadership*. New York: Simon and Schuster.

O'Hair, D. & Friedrich, G.W. (1992). *Strategic communication in business and the professions.* Boston: MA: Houghton Mifflin.

Paulis, P., Seta, C. & Baron, R (1996). *Effective human relations.* Boston: Allyn and Bacon.

Pace, R. W. & Faules, D. F. (1994). *Organizational communication* (3rd ed.). Englewood Cliffs, NJ: Prentice Hall.

Parker, G. M. (1991). *Team players and teamwork.* San Francisco: Jossey Bass.

Parker, L. E., & Price, R. H. (1994). Empowered managers and empowered workers: The effects of managerial support and managerial perceived control on workers' sense of control over decision making. *Human Relations, 47* (8), 911-928.

Patton, T. H. (1981). *Organizational development through teambuilding.* New York: Wiley.

Pelz, D.C. (1952). Influence: A key to effective leadership in the first-line supervisor. *Personnel, 29,* 3-11.

Pfeffer, J. (1992). *Managing with power.* Boston: Harvard Business School.

Poole, M. S. (1985). Communication and organizational climates: Review, critique and a new perspective. In R.D. McPhee & P.K. Tomkins (Eds.) *Organizational communication: Traditional themes and new directions* (pp. 79-108). Beverly Hills, CA: Sage.

Popcorn, F. (1991). *The popcorn report.* New York: Currency and Doubleday.

Redding, W.C. (1972). *Communication wihtin the organizaiton: An interpretive review of theory and research.* New York: Industrial Communcation Council.

Rhodes, S.C. (1987). A study of effective and ineffective dyads using the systems theory principle of entropy. *Journal of International Listening Association, 1,* 43-49.

Roethlishberger, F. (1988). Barriers and gateways to communication. In G. Manning and K. Curtis (Eds.) *Communication: The miracle of dialogue* (pp. 192-202). Cincinnati: Southwestern.

Rogers, C. (1990). Experiences in communication. In J. Stewart (Ed.) *Bridges not walls* (pp. 438-444). New York: McGraw Hill.

Rokeach, M. (1960). *The open and closed mind.* New York: Basic Books.

Rose, F. (1989). *West of Eden: The end of innocence at Apple Computer.* New York: Viking Press.

Rosenfeld, L. B. (1983). Communication climate and coping mechanisms in the college classroom. *Communication Education, 34,* 167-174.

Rossiter, C.M. & Pearce, W.B. (1975). *Communicating personally: A theory of interpersonal communication and human relationships.* Indianapolis: Bobbs-Merrill.

Royal, K. E., & Austin, J. (1992). Evaluation of an hypothetical company recruiter by management by management students. *Psychological Reports, 70* (1), 89-90.

Sanders, R. (1995). A new rhetorical perspective: The enactment of role identities as interactive strategies. In S. Sigman (Ed.) *The consequentiality of communication* (pp. 67-120). Hillsdale, NJ: Lawrence Erlbaum.

Schein, E. H. (1985). *Organizational culture and leadership.* San Francisco: Jossey Bass.

Schindler, P. L. & Thomas, C. C. (1993). The structure of interpersonal trust in the workplace. *Psychological Reports*, 73 (2), 563-573.

Seers, A., Petty, M. M., and Cashman, J. F. (1995). Team-members exchange under team and traditional management: A naturally occurring quasi-experiment. *Group and Organizational Management*, 20 (1), 18-38.

Seligman, M. (1988, October). Boomer blues. *Psychology Today*, p. 50-55.

Senge, P. M. (1980). The leader's new work: Building learning organizations. *Sloan Management Review*,. 3-14.

Senge, P. M. (1990). *The fifth discipline*. New York: Doubleday.

Sherman, S. (1993, January 25). A brave new Darwinian workplace. *Fortune*, 50-56.

Sieberg, E. (1985). *Family communication*. New York: Gardner Press.

Smith, R.C. and Eisenberg, E. M. (1987) Conflict at disneyland: A root-metaphor analysis. *Communication Monographs*, 54, 367-380.

Solomon, L. J., BrehoNew York, K. A., Rothblum, E. D. & Kelly, J. A. (1982). Corporate managers' reactions to assertive social skills exhibited by males and females. *Journal of Organizational Behavior Management*, 4 (3-4), 49-63.

Some companies cut costs too far, suffer "corporate anorexia." (1995, July 5). *Wall Street Journal*, p.1

Spangle, M. & Knapp, D. (1996). The effectiveness of debate as a corporate decision making tool. *The Southern Journal of Forensics*, 1 (3).

Spitzberg, B. H. (1988). Communication competence: Measures of perceived effectiveness. In Charles H. Tardy (Ed.), *A Handbook for the study of human communication* (pp. 67-105). Norwood, NJ: Ablex.

Spitzberg, B. H. & Hurt, H.T. (1987). The measurement of interpersonal skills in instructional contexts. *Communication Education*, 36, 28-45.

Sproull, L. & Kiesler, S. (1991, September). Computers, networks, and work. *Scientific American*, 265, 116-123.

Stahl, D. (1989, March). Managing in the 1990's: Versatility, flexibility and a wide range of skills. A new study outlines the requirements for managerial success in a complex and fast-changing business world. *A T & T Journal*, 8-10.

Stewart, J. & Thomas, M. (1990). Dialogic listening: Sculpting mutual meanings. In J. Stewart (Ed.) *Bridges not walls* (5th ed.) (pp. 192-210). New York: McGraw-Hill.

Stewart, P.W. (1993). A suprising union? A soft systems analysis and sociometry. In F.A. Stowell, D. West, & J.D. Howell (Eds.) *Systems Science*. New York: Bantam Books.

Stewart, R. (1967). *Managers and their jobs*. London: Macmillan.

Stewart, T. (1991, August 12). GE keep those ideas coming. *Fortune*, p. 41.

Stiff, J.B., Dillard, J.P., Somera, L., Kim, H. & Sleight, C. (1988). Empathy, communication, and prosocial behavior. *Communication Monographs*, 55, 198-213.

Tichy. N. and Charan, R. (1993). Speed, simplicity, self confidence: An interview with Jack Welch. *In Articulate Executive* (221-237). Boston: Harvard Business Review.

Tjosvold, D. *Teamwork for customers: Building organizations that take pride in serving*. San Francisco: Jossey-Bass.

Towers, J. (1996). In M. Marquardt *Building the Learning Organization*. New York: McGraw-Hill, p.193.

Trenholm, S. (1986). *Human communication theory*. Englewood Cliffs, N.J.: Prentice Hall.

Tubbs, S. L. & Moss, S. (1994). *Human communication* (7th ed.). New York: McGraw-Hill.

Ugbah, S. D., & Dewine, S. (1989). New communication technologiea: The impact on intra- organizational dynamics. *Information & Management*, 17 (3), 181-186.

Ury, W. (1991). *Getting past no*. New York: Bantam.

Verderber, R. & Verderber, K. (1995). *Inter-act: Using personal communication skills*(7th ed.). Belmont, CA: Wadsworth.

Waldron, V. (1991). Achieving goals in superior-subordinate relationships: The multifunctionality of upward maintenance tactics. *Communication Monographs*, 58, 280-306.

Walton, D. (1988). *Are you communicating?* New York: McGraw Hill.

Watzlawick, Bavelas & Jackson. (1967). *Pragmatics of human communication*. New York: W. W. Norton.

Weaver, R. (1987). *Understanding human communication*. Glenview, IL: Foresman and Co.

Welter, P. (1978). *How to help a friend*. Wheaton, ILL: Tyndale House.

Wick, C. and Leon, L.S. (1993). *The learning edge: How smart companies and smart managers stay ahead*. New York: McGraw-Hill.

Wiemann, J. (1977). Explication and test of a model of communication competence. *Human Communication Research*, 3, 195-213.

Wilmot, W. W. & Baxter, L. (1989). The relationship schemata model: On linking communication
  with relationships. Paper presented at Western States Speech Communication Association
  Convention,, Spokane, WA.

Wilson. G.L., Hantz, A.M. & Hanna, M.S. (1995). *Interpersonal communication*. Dubuque, IA: Brown
  and Benchmark.

Wolvin, A.D. & Coakley, C.G. (1985). *Listening*. Dubuque, IA: Brown.

1995 industry report (1995, October). *Training*, p. 37-77.

Index